Continuity of Norwegian Tradition
in the Pacific Northwest

Henning K. Sehmsdorf

Copyright 2020 S&S Homestead Press
First printing by Applied Digital Imaging Inc, Bellingham, WA
Second printing by IngramSpark, La Vergne, TN
ISBN 9798985127713

Cover: 1925 U.S. postage stamp celebrating the centennial of the 54 ft (39 ton) sloop "Restauration" arriving in New York City, carrying 52 mostly Norwegian Quakers from Stavanger, Norway to the New World.

Table of Contents

Preface

For the more than three decades I taught Scandinavian studies at the University of Washington in Seattle, I witnessed a lively Norwegian American community celebrating its ethnic heritage, though no more than approximately 1.5% of self-declared Norwegian Americans, a mere fraction of the approximately 280,000 Americans of Norwegian descent living in Washington State today, claim membership in ethnic organizations such as the Sons of Norway. At musical events and dances at *Leikarringen* and folk dance summer camps; salmon dinners and traditional Christmas celebrations at Leif Ericsson Lodge; cross-country skiing at *Trollhaugen* near Stampede Pass; historical and contemporary exhibits at the Nordic Heritage Museum; language instruction at the Scandinavian Language Institute, and classes in folk crafts and cuisine at the Scandinavian Cultural Center at Pacific Lutheran University, and elsewhere; Midsummer festivities at Poulsbo and *Syttende Mai* (Norwegian Constitution Day) parades in every large and small community in the Pacific Northwest wherever Norwegians had settled during the great emigration to America between the middle of the nineteenth century and the nineteen thirties — Norwegian Americans gave expression to their love of the traditions of the country from which their forebears emigrated as early as two hundred years ago.

During the 1980s when I was teaching a fieldwork-based course on Nordic folk belief and world view, I sent my students to find story and material traditions still alive and passed on between first and third or fourth generations of Norwegian Americans in the Pacific Northwest. At the waterfront in Seattle, we met retired fishermen who told us about the history of the fishing industry in the Pacific Northwest spearheaded by Norwegian immigrants. Among them we discovered a remarkable storyteller, Fred Simonsen, and recorded twelve of his personal narratives before he died that year. To our surprise, we also found three boat builders who still constructed wooden boats in the ancient Viking tradition, and we discovered that some of the ancient beliefs circumscribing the world view of farmers, fishermen and others in pre-industrial Norway were still remembered by some Norwegian Americans. The results of this field work found their way into articles published in *Northwest Folklore* and in ethnographic journals in Norway and Germany.

About a generation ago, I left the University to run the family farm on Lopez Island and teach about regenerative agriculture. Now in my eighties, I have reconnected with the Norwegian community to take a fresh look at the continuity of Norwegian traditions in the Northwest. Since last November, I have interviewed more than half a hundred Norwegian Americans mostly in the Seattle area, but also elsewhere in Washington and Oregon. What I found is that by and large the ancient beliefs of an earlier immigrant generation, about the human soul and about the interactions between people and nature spirits have disappeared, and most people today live in the binary world of the Enlightenment that has come down to us mostly through industrialization, commerce and modern media. Part of the reason is that the majority of Norwegian Americans no longer speak, read or write the language of their immigrant ancestors and now live in the mental world circumscribed by English. However, I also found that Norwegian Americans continue to take great pride in their ethnic heritage, partly perhaps because of their participation in folkloric events: dancing, fiddle playing, choral singing, woodworking, weaving and sewing crafts, cooking, baking and seasonal celebrations, all of which provide a sense of community, a cultural home missing in much of contemporary, commercially and technologically driven, urban life. Norwegian Americans cherish the artifacts of the culture of their immigrant past for their unique fusion of function and form which they find beautiful and worthy of celebration and commemoration. A few still build those beautiful Viking-style boats, for example, even though these are no longer used for fishing, but for tourist activities and youth programs. Beyond that, however, I also found a remarkable degree of participation in this cultural celebration of Norway's heritage by non-Norwegians: dancers and musicians at *Leikarringen* and in musical groups that fuse traditions from various backgrounds; young people of many ethnic backgrounds learning to play the Hardanger fiddle and the music identified with that proto-Norwegian instrument; food consumers seeking out traditional delicacies at Scandinavian Specialties in Ballard or similar stores elsewhere; people shopping for Norwegian furniture such as the famous *Ekornes* armchairs for their durable beauty and quality craftsmanship; or the Young Nordics, a group of professionals formed at the Nordic Heritage Museum, foregrounding the vibrant, and increasingly diverse, cultural life in Norway today. A stunning fusion of traditional and modern Norwegian culture can be found in the work of some American silversmiths in Seattle who, after extended study and practice of their craft in Norway, have developed new forms of jewelry in which facets of the old, rural culture of Norway live on in the new, urban culture of America.

Some of the people I queried about continuity of Norwegian tradition in Seattle today, emphasized that while the majority of Norwegian Americans no longer seek out the traditional folk culture of their origin, Norwegian and other Scandinavian immigrants have left a permanent imprint on Seattle and Northwest culture. In a recent article by Knute Berger (a third generation Norwegian American), Kristine Leander, head of Seattle's Swedish Club, identified important traits in Seattle culture she believes stem from Scandinavia: a tendency for people to be "publicly friendly, yet very private;" a love of *hygge,* "a kind of coziness amid nature that is seen as a virtue;" and the much criticized, participatory "Seattle process," where "everyone wants a say, and decisions don't necessarily come easily." Berger also maintains that the socially democratic tendencies increasingly resonating in the city, have Scandinavian antecedents, a view I found echoed among several people I interviewed. Berger quotes Peter Jackson, son of famous Norwegian American senator, "Scoop" Jackson: "Is it ironic that Seattle's reflection of Norse political culture is inversely proportional to the local Norse population? We're all Norwegians now."[1]

I wish to take the opportunity to thank all the informants who patiently filled out my traditions questionnaire, sat for recorded interviews and answered follow-up questions. Among these, I especially want to note boat builders Jay Smith and Paul Schweiss; long-time director of *Leikarringen,* Larry Reinert; Hardanger fiddle players Bill Boyd and Rachel Nesvig; violin and Hardanger fiddle maker Lynn Berg; director of *Lilla Spelmanslaget* Martha Levenson; director of Scandinavian Language Institute Ed Egerdahl and his students; musician, recording artist and author Beth Sankey Kollé; co-editor (with Beth Kollé) of the *Songbook for the Daughters of Norway,* Janet Ruud; Textile Curator and Collections Manager at the Scandinavian Cultural Center at Pacific Lutheran University, Linda Caspersen; *bunad*-expert Jody Grage; silver

---

[1] Berger, Knute 2018. "A New Generation is Embracing Seattle's Nordic History & Culture," *Seattle Magazine*; see also Leander, Kristine 2008. *Norwegian Seattle.* Arcadia Publishing Library Editions.

smiths Lori Talcott and Felicia Bauer; storyteller Kirsten Quistad and other former students at the University of Washington: Gry Løklingholm, Lars Jenner, and Kari Gunvaldsen Swanson, some of whom were part of the original traditions study in the 1980-1990s; Jens Lund, former director of the Washington Folklife Council; and my Norwegian American neighbors on Lopez Island, where I live. Without their enthusiasm for this project, the rich tapestry of information they provided and patient edits of what I wrote, this book would never have seen the light of day. I express my deep appreciation.

Henning Sehmsdorf, Lopez Island, WA, 2020.

Continuity of Norwegian Traditions in the Pacific Northwest[1]

Immigration

May 17 Parade in Ballard 2019. Photo by author.

A number of years ago, on a brilliantly sunny day, I was marching in a parade in Ballard, a traditionally Norwegian district of Seattle. It was May 17, the anniversary of the day in 1814 when Norway declared its independence from Denmark and adopted its own constitution. In Seattle, Norwegian Constitution Day has been a public celebration since 1889, the central event of which is the parade, a parade second in size and popularity only to the annual Seafair Parade organized by the fishing and boating industry.

Looking around, I saw thousands of people lining the streets, shouting and singing and waving Norwegian and American flags. I was marching side by side with a friend of mine, an exchange professor from the University of Bergen in Norway. My friend was obviously impressed by the size and enthusiasm of the crowd, but also a little bewildered. This parade was not like any May 17 celebration he had experienced in Norway. Where were the patriotic slogans and exhortations by city fathers and politicians? Wasn't anyone going to sing the Norwegian national anthem or shout "Long live the King"? Instead of the joyous solemnity typical of the celebration in the "old country," the 17th of May in Seattle feels like an American carnival. Beside marchers in Norwegian costume, there are teams of Black breakdancers, Hispanic drill teams, Japanese marching bands, Bavarian yodelers, clowns, Boy Scouts and Shriners, colorful floats advertising their commercial sponsors; mingled in the crowd, there are hucksters selling hot dogs and soft drinks; and shops and cafes along the parade route enjoy a brisk business. To the people of Seattle, May 17 is probably what St. Patrick's Day is to New Yorkers: people are getting together for a public party to celebrate not so much the independence of Norway (or, for that matter, the arrival of the missionary saint to the shores of Ireland), as to celebrate that they are Americans of distinct ethnic backgrounds.

Next to Ireland, no nation in Europe sent a larger portion of its population to America than did Norway. Few came before 1820, and before

1840 Norwegians were not permitted to emigrate without specific consent from the monarch. In 1825 fifty-two Quakers and Haugeans from Stavanger crossed the Atlantic aboard the "Restauration" (The Restoration), and by 1860 only 6,000 souls had followed their example. But by 1910 the U.S. census calculated that some 800,000 Norwegians had emigrated, leaving only twice that many people behind in the "old country." By 1920 the Norwegian Bureau of Statistics showed that there were 1.2 million people of "unmixed Norwegian descent" living in the U.S., including those born in the U.S. of Norwegian parents. Most of the earliest Norwegian immigrants settled as farmers in the Midwest and in Texas. By the time larger groups reached the Pacific Northwest, most of the available land had already been homesteaded, and the Norwegians were forced to settle marginal areas where the soil was thin or rainfall scarce. Some of the immigrants, however, were able to find good land in, for instance, the Skagit

Valley around Stanwood and Sylvana; others were able to buy out existing homesteads, in, for example, the Palouse area of Eastern Washington; others pushed on to the West Coast and Alaska to work as fishermen, or found jobs in the burgeoning cities, notably Seattle. By 1920, the year when Scandinavian

Memorial stone, Stanwood Cemetery. Photo by the author.

immigration to the Pacific Northwest was at its peak, there were nearly 10,000 native Norwegians in Seattle, comprising about 1/6 to 1/8 of the foreign-born settled in the city.[2] Remarkably, the first white person born in the 18th century to settle in the Stillaquamish Valley was Norwegian Emerenze Toftezen who sailed around Cape Horn and reached the Pacific Northwest in

1849. She and other Norwegian settlers are commemorated in the cemetery in Stanwood, where Crown Prince Olav deposited flowers in 1939. By 1990, 32.5% of all Norwegian Americans were settled in the West, with the State of Washington boasting 333,521 Norwegian Americans or 6.85% of the total state population, ranking fourth after Minnesota, Wisconsin and California.[3]

Assimilation and Adaptation

For a time after the Norwegians arrived in the area, they tried to retain their cultural identity. They lived in tightly knit communities such as Ballard (now part of Seattle); Selbu in Eastern Washington, named after a village in Western Norway; "Snus Hill" (Snoose Hill) near Bellingham in Western Washington, named for the Norwegians' supposed habit of dipping snuff; and Sylvana in the Skagit Valley. Norwegian was spoken at home, at school and in church, and a network of Norwegian language publications was established (of which *Western Viking,* started in 1889 under its former name, *Washington Posten,* survived until 2006, and is today continued as *The Norwegian American*). The Norwegian Lutheran Church, which by the 1880s had founded Norwegian language theological seminaries and colleges in the Midwest, extended its organization to the Pacific Northwest. Pacific Lutheran University in Tacoma, for example, was founded as a denominational college. Until about ten years ago, the former First Norwegian Lutheran church in Seattle (now Denny Park Lutheran) offered regular services in Norwegian.[4] Ballard First Lutheran continues to offer a Christmas Day service in English and Norwegian.[5]

By the eve of World War I, however, Norwegian communities already faced pressures from various quarters to assimilate with the English-speaking populations around them. Theodore Roosevelt, for example, sternly criticized any effort on the part of immigrants to keep alive their native language and culture. In an address he gave in New York in 1915, the former President said:

The one absolutely certain way of bringing this nation to ruin would be to permit it to become a tangle of squabbling nationalities, an intricate knot of German-Americans, Irish-Americans, English-Americans, French-Americans, Scandinavian-Americans or Italian-Americans, each preserving its separate nationality, each at heart feeling more sympathy with Europeans of that nationality than with other citizens of the American Republic. The men who do not become Americans and nothing else are hyphenated Americans; and there ought to be no room for them in this country.

Instead, foreign born citizens were urged to adopt "a common language, English; [and] a common civil standard, similar ideals, beliefs and customs symbolized by the oath of allegiance to America."[6]

Roosevelt's crusade against so-called "hyphenism," while understandable from the perspective of national security in war times, confused the issues of civic loyalty and cultural orientation, and caused much anxiety among Norwegian Americans who felt increasingly compelled to assimilate. Other factors contributing to this trend were technological and economic, rather than political. In the 1920s, telephones and radios brought the "outside" (i.e., English-speaking) world into Norwegian American homes, while a decade later automobiles carried the next generation off to the large cities to look for jobs. The Great Depression of the 1930s and the renewed emphasis on civic loyalty during the Second World War further accelerated assimilation.

In the Pacific Northwest, the period during which Norwegian immigrants were able to live within their own cultural context was thus relatively brief. The trend toward complete integration into American life continued until the late 1950-1960s.[7] However, many second, third, and fourth generation Norwegian Americans, firmly part of the cultural mainstream and usually well educated and economically secure, renewed contact with the culture of their forefathers. Ethnic organizations, such as the Sons of Norway, now no longer focus on immigrants, but on heritage programs to keep alive memories of "how things were."[8] Such programs usually include traditional arts and crafts — notably rose painting, Hardanger stitchery and weaving — travelogs, courses in genealogy designed to help families trace their Norwegian ancestry, classes in language, cooking and folk dance, summer camps for children and adolescents, choral groups, and other social activities.

Concomitantly, there has been a steadily increasing interest in the study of Scandinavian languages and cultures at the college level. Over several years, I encouraged students in the Scandinavian Department at the University of Washington to interview immigrants from Norway to this area, most of whom were then in their seventies and eighties, as well as the children and grandchildren of these immigrants. Analysis of this material confirms that for the majority of Norwegian Americans the most important function of their shared heritage is to give them a sense of identity and belonging. They take pride in being "American," and put a high value on what they regard as central American virtues such as neighborliness, friendliness, and individual initiative and enterprise. However, when I raised the question of world view in a recent round of inquiry, one Norwegian immigrant identified what she considered an essential Norwegian virtue expressed in the social democracies of the Nordic countries: politicians, the media and the public working together to improve socio-economic conditions for everyone.[9] But over and above that, most Norwegian immigrants and their American descendants cherish traditions that are specific to the material culture of their ethnic origin — mostly food ways, housing and furnishing styles, crafts, holiday and outdoor activities such as boating, fishing, hiking, and skiing. It comes as no surprise that Norwegian organizations maintain ski jumps and cross-country trails and a well-equipped mountain lodge appropriately named *Trollhaugen* (Troll Hill) near Seattle, something we would find astonishing in the case of, for example, Japanese or Mexican Americans, to name just two other major ethnic minorities in the Puget Sound area.

Storied Tradition

As folklorist Gerald Cashion points out, tradition manifests in many oral and verbal forms ("mentifacts:" world view, belief, story), kinesiological forms ("sociofacts:" dance, music, singing, culinary and craft practices), and in material forms ("artifacts:" instruments, clothing, foods, craft products, boats, and more). A tradition lives on in its performance as people interact with one another.[10]

Belief & Story: The hundreds of thousands of Norwegians settled in America by the end of the nineteenth century, stepped from the Old World in which nature was seen as alive and endowed with spirit into a New World where nature was regarded as a "demonic" wilderness to be conquered, or as a resource to be "developed." In the immigrants' home country the invisible powers of nature had been thought to live side by side with human beings, the work rhythms and daily needs of both groups overlapping in many ways, and the protection and welfare of the farmhouse and its immediate surroundings had found expression in traditions about guardian beings called variously *tomte* ("homestead man"), *gardvord* ("farm guardian"), and *tunkall* ("yard fellow"), each name stressing the identification of this protective being with the farmstead.[11] This view of nature as alive and endowed with spirit in many ways echoed the world view of the native populations the Norwegian settlers encountered, for example, in the Dakota prairies. Sitting Bull, the famous Lakota chief who defeated Custer at Little Big Horn in 1876, for instance, is said to have described the continuity between the human and natural environments as follows: "Every seed is awakened and so is all animal life. It is through this mysterious power that we have our being and we therefore yield to our animal neighbors."[12] The newcomers, however, had little opportunity to realize the affinity between their own world view and that of the native inhabitants of the land the immigrants were claiming for themselves. Ever since the Puritans, nature and the natives living there had been demonized by the religious, "because nature, since Eden, had been corrupted by human sin."[13] From the start, the Puritans saw it "as their God-ordained destiny to transform the dismal American wilderness into an earthly paradise, governed according to the Word of God."[14] The view of nature as demonic and evil, of course, was also promoted by the Norwegian church which decried any belief in nature spirits as pagan, and this ecclesiastic attitude carried over into the conservative Norwegian synod established on American soil in 1853.[15] It is also reflected in the ambiguous portrayal of the minister and church authority in folk belief, custom, legend and folktale.[16] Thus, upon emigration from their communities, the settlers found themselves uprooted not only from the homesteads and families they had left behind in their native country, but also from the traditional feeling of being embedded in a natural environment they could understand and trust; instead they found themselves thrust into a demonic wilderness populated by strange animals and devilish Indians. The master chronicler of the Norwegian settlement of the American Midwest, Ole Rölvaag, captured this sense of cultural estrangement in the tragic figure of Beret, wife of Per Hansa, a natural pioneer who saw nothing but the promise of the American frontier, while she was driven to insanity by her incurable fear of a demonic and hostile natural environment:

> When the others had gone and the children were asleep, Beret rose and hung some heavy clothes up over the windows — the thickest clothes she could find — to shut out the night. She felt that she could never go to bed, with all the eyes out there, staring in upon her ...
> ...Last of all, she pulled the big chest in front of the door.[17]

However, some of the old beliefs surrounding nature and the human self, and of the church's response to those beliefs, did survive the long process of cultural assimilation, and more than a century later, remnants of the pre-industrial world view could still be found among Norwegian immigrants and their descendants. The interviews I carried out with my students in the 1980-1990s, revealed some fascinating survivals of belief traditions that were brought here by the immigrants and in some instances continued to structure reality for them, and their descendants, in tangible ways. For example, in 1981 a woman in her late fifties who had grown up on a farm in northern Norway and now lived on a farm near Seattle, told us that she was afraid of black dogs because she had seen the devil in dog shape when she was a girl; nor did she like talking about black dogs because she might inadvertently call upon the devil.[18] A second immigrant we interviewed, also living in Seattle, was convinced that whenever her husband or sons returned home from work or school, she knew of their arrival fifteen minutes or so before they actually walked through the door, because of what she called the *vardøyger* (premonitory sound or vision). According to traditional Norwegian folk belief, the *vardøyger* is a manifestation of a person's mind which precedes him or her to announce their approach.[19] My informant told me that she would hear the sounds usually associated with the arrival of her husband or sons; and then she would know it was time to put on the coffee or the evening meal. She was surprised to find out that Americans didn't know about this and wondered how they managed their households.[20]

Another woman, age sixty-six, who was born in North Dakota of Norwegian parents and later moved to Seattle, had learned in her childhood that illness or socially unacceptable behavior was caused by being possessed by someone else's *hug*, which was the traditional term for mind or thought.[21] When she was a child, there was usually someone in her own family who knew how to drive the *hug* from an afflicted person or animal. The traditional procedure was to cup one's hand over the ear of the patient and then shout *Ho! Ho! Har du Finn hug?* (literally, do you have a Finn's mind or, more loosely translated, "Has someone hexed you by sending malevolent thoughts?"[22]

The informant remembered that when she was about five, her sixteen-year-old sister applied this treatment to a cow which wouldn't stand still for the milking. But she also remembered that the ritual was cut short when the younger children tattled to their parents, who apparently thought that the traditional cure was out of place in America.

Another experience recalled by the same informant had to do with omens of death. According to traditional belief in Norway, a person's *hug* would make its presence felt to faraway loved ones at the moment of death. In 1938, the informant's mother died suddenly in North Dakota. By that time, her aunt had moved to Everett and her brother to Longview, both in Washington State. When the brother called the aunt to inform her that her sister had passed away, she already knew about it: she had heard three knocks on the door of her house at the hour of the woman's death.

Similarly, in 1978, a neighbor of mine, an elderly Norwegian woman whom I knew only as "Lettie," came to talk to me in my backyard where I was chopping wood.[23] Her husband and her only son had died several years before, and the woman lived alone and rarely spoke to anyone. Her visit surprised me, but she was agitated and said she needed to talk to someone. That morning, while she was drinking coffee in her kitchen, her husband and son had appeared to her; she hadn't actually seen them, but they had sat next to her and spoken to her, saying that they wanted her to come with them. I just listened, knowing that according to Norwegian tradition, the dead could send their *hug* to communicate with the living. It struck me that Lettie had experienced an omen of her own death. She passed away a few days later.

Another informant, an immigrant from northern Norway, had come to Seattle in 1960 to be married, when she was fifty-three years of age.[24] As a young woman, while she was training as a nurse, she got a bad case of warts on both her hands, and neither medications nor treatment with electric needles by a regular physician helped. Then she met a man in Hammerfest who offered to cure her. He tied as many knots in a piece of string as there were warts on her hands, and then he buried the string in a place "where the sun never shines," by which he meant on the north side of a cliff. Although the young nurse did not believe in the efficacy of this magical cure, less than two weeks later the warts were gone completely and so were the scars left by the electric needles. She wondered about this a lot, but later on when she was working as a nurse in a hospital, she met a young man who had warts that were as "big as a cauliflower"; she used the same technique, tying knots in a string, and again it worked.

Later, when the informant was working as a medical assistant in Seattle taking blood tests, a Norwegian patient claimed that he was a blood-stopper, meaning that he knew how to stop bleeding magically. She challenged him to teach her, and he returned a few days later to ask her why she wanted to learn, and whether she was willing to keep it a secret if he entrusted her with his power. He then taught her the following:

Say the name of your patient, then command his blood to stop, pronouncing the following words:

I den samme Jordans flod
som Jesus døptes god,
stenger jeg dit blod.

(In the same Jordan river
in which Jesus was baptized,
I stay your blood).

Then you add: *In the name of the Father, the Son, and the Holy Ghost,* and pray the Lord's Prayer three times.

This blood-stopper was a faith healer; there are many active in Norway even now.[25] The formula he taught to the informant is well known. It is based upon an apocryphal Biblical tradition according to which the river Jordan stopped flowing when Jesus stepped into the water to be baptized. By invoking the formula, the healer establishes a sympathetic relationship between the sacred power of Christ and himself. Channeling this power to the patient, he drives out the hostile force (*hug*) which is causing the bleeding. When the interviewer asked the informant whether she had ever made use of the formula herself, she answered no, "Because there were doctors around; but if I had been far away from doctors, up in the mountains, and there was real danger, then I would have used it."

Three other informants I want to mention here are retired fishermen. The first, A.K. Larson,[26] was well known in the Norwegian community in the Puget Sound area. He was in his early twenties when he came to Seattle in 1936 and at that time, he said, "90 to 95% of all halibut fishermen on the West Coast were Norwegians." In fact, the "entire deep sea industry was dominated by Norwegians." Larson wrote a couple of books about fishing and fishing boats, and he was an active member of the Deep Sea Fisherman's Union for many years. In the late 1950s when halibut fishing went belly up due to overfishing both by domestic and foreign boats, Larson went to work for The Fisheries Research Institute at the University of Washington, then for the U.S. Bureau of Fisheries in Alaska; in 1963 the National Science Foundation sent him to India as an advisor for fisheries. It is interesting to hear a man of Larson's knowledge and experience say that most fishermen of his generation were superstitious. As he put it, "The dangerous things are old and tried; you must never mention a pig or a horse on a boat, otherwise there will be bad weather or gear will be lost overboard. A black suitcase is bad, but a black umbrella is deadly."

Similar examples were provided by another fisherman, Einar Pedersen,[27] who described an incident when his father made the ship's cook throw his black suitcase overboard because it was storming. Black galoshes or black umbrellas were never allowed on board, said Pedersen, nor was it permitted for sailors to whistle while manning the helm, lest "you whistle up a wind." Pedersen also related the story of how his uncle turned back to port because black seagoing birds the informant called shags, were flying against the direction in which the boat was going. By contrast, in 1985, a third informant,[28] when asked about similar superstitions, claimed that he had never set any store by them. "Knowledge of what you are doing is what counts," was his belief, squarely reflecting the pragmatism of Americans. For many Norwegian Americans, however, what remains of the old beliefs even today is a generalized "spiritual" sense of nature,[29] a deep feeling of connectedness with sea and forest linked to their ethnic identity.[30]

Ethnic Jokes, Personal Narratives, and Sayings: In 2020, when I surveyed new informants about traditional Norwegian folk beliefs, the responses showed consistently that such beliefs no longer structured their view of the world in existentially significant ways. Perhaps the survey sample was too small, but I doubt it: both in Norway and in the U.S., the pre-industrial world view based on an assumed intimacy between nature and human beings has been replaced by an objective relationship in which nature is understood at best as "environment" or, more problematically, as "resource." The pathologies of "nature-deficiency" and climate change result from this shift. Norwegian traditions of nature spirits continue, however, in commercial applications such Thor comics, computer trolls, or children's fantasy stories, including bowdlerized editions of Norwegian folktales.[31]

While Norwegian belief traditions have not survived immigrant assimilation, the traditions of telling ethnic stories, jokes and popular sayings, however, are thriving. "Ole & Lena (or Sven)" jokes are ubiquitous wherever Norwegian Americans gather socially.[32] Here are a couple of examples:

Ole and Sven are sitting on the porch and talking when Sven looks down at Ole's feet and says: "Do you know your socks don't match? One is red and the other is blue." Ole said: "Ja, I really like them and I have another pair just like them in my drawer at home."

Ole died. His wife Lena went to the local newspaper to place an obituary. The man at the paper said: "What do you want us to write?" Lena said: "Ole Died." The man said: "Is that all? If it's money you're worried about, the first five words are free."

So, Lena thought for a while, then she smiled and said: "OK, then write: "Ole Died, Boat for Sale."[33]

An ethnic joke I collected from one of my students in the 1980s still circulates among Norwegian Americans in Seattle which, in my opinion, tells a great deal about how this group perceives itself today:[34]

There was an exchange student from Norway who wanted to join an American college fraternity. As a condition of membership, the fraternity challenged him to a test. They showed him three tents. In the first there was a bottle of aquavit, in the second a grizzly bear with an abscessed tooth, and in the third a beautiful sorority girl. Empty that bottle of aquavit in one draught, they said; then pull the grizzly's tooth, and finally, make love to the girl three times, and do it all in one hour. Well, that Norwegian, he gulped down the aquavit. By the time he entered the second tent, he was a bit unsteady on his feet. Then there were great crashing noises, and howls and curses; and by the time the Norwegian emerged from that tent, he was bleeding and his clothes were torn. But he had a triumphant look in his eyes, and shouted: "Uff da, where is that girl with the abscessed tooth?"

Norwegian American folklorist Jan Harold Brunvand has reported a large number of fraternity initiation stories in his books on modern urban legends in America, but to my knowledge this one is not among them, yet. In an article published in 1960, however, Brunvand documents that the story of the greenhorn who is put to a series of three or four tests before being accepted as a peer, has been recorded by folklorists in Alaska four times between 1947 and 1959, and in the latter year a graduate student in folklore at Indiana University reported a version containing the same three tasks included in the Seattle variant: the initiate must empty a fifth of whiskey at one draught, wrestle with a grizzly bear and sleep with an (Eskimo) woman; after successfully downing the whiskey, he confuses the bear and the woman. It is interesting that at the same time this joke was circulating in Alaska, it was also reported from northern Norway, where it seems to have been well known among sailors and fishermen, and also among children. A variant collected there from a 10-year old boy and printed in the fisherman's magazine *Skip Ahoi!"* in 1959, describes a sailor's apprentice on his first trip to Greenland. His initiation into manhood involves emptying a bottle of aquavit, wrestling a polar bear into submission, and raping an Eskimo woman. He nearly succeeds, but loses the wrestling match with the Eskimo woman.[35]

It appears likely that this initiation story is yet another oral tradition brought to the Pacific Northwest by Norwegian immigrants, perhaps in the 1940-1950s, and survives among Norwegian Americans in the area today. The cruder sexual chauvinism of the older version aside, both variants celebrate traditional qualities of maleness: the ability to hold large quantities of liquor, physical strength, and sexual prowess. Both variants also poke fun at the initiate, the greenhorn. But there is a striking difference between the two variants. While in the older story the butt of the joke is the initiate, the young sailor-to-be, in the Seattle version it is the Norwegian precisely because he *is* Norwegian. In other words, the Seattle version functions as an ethnic joke. The joke pokes fun at certain characteristics Norwegian Americans identify with the culture of their own origin, namely that Norwegians supposedly are naive and gullible: "blue-eyed," as they say.

Another well known Norwegian ethnic joke was recently told to me by a retired Lutheran pastor on Lopez Island, who heard it from a Swedish colleague:

There's this older couple on our island who one day discovered that a pair of sea otters had settled below their porch. And, man, did they stink! So a Norwegian friend gave them this advice: "Put a bunch

Descendants of emigrants from Norway. 1925 photo by Fenney. Minnesota Historical

of *lutefisk* under the porch, that'll drive the otters out for sure." Well they did, and it worked! But when their friend asked them how it went with the *lutefisk*, they answered, "We got rid of the otters alright, but now we have a family of Norwegians living under the porch!"[36]

Sociologist Herbert Gans labels ethnic jokes as "symbolic ethnicity." An ethnic group such as Norwegian Americans who feel secure about their place in the American mainstream can afford humorous self-ridicule in later generations, once they are freed from the constraints of their ethnic background and culture.[37]

Personal experience narratives are another ethnic genre broadly represented in the Norwegian American community. Like other ethnic groups, Norwegian Americans enjoy telling the stories of their own or their ancestors' immigration and experiences in America, their memories of the "old country," genealogies, families, friends and places left behind, or reconnected with during visits to Norway. For instance, in 1925 the descendants of the Quakers from Stavanger who a century earlier escaped suppression by the Lutheran Church by emigrating, gathered to have their picture taken before a life-size replica of the *Restauration,* and no doubt exchanged historical accounts and personal narratives, remembering why they left their native country, their ninety-two day journey on a fifty-four foot sloop of no more than forty-five tons, bearing dramatic witness to their intrepid faith as well as to the traditional boat building and seafaring skills of Norway.[38]

Sometimes, personal narratives rise to the level of polished set-pieces and the teller earns a reputation by performing regularly at given venues. One such storyteller in Seattle was Fred Simonsen (1890-1990), a retired fisherman living in Ballard, who had been telling stories since his retirement in 1960. Simonsen was never a church-goer, and thus the church community which otherwise plays a central role in Norwegian American tradition, was

Deep-sea halibut fishing in open dories, 1920-1930s. Museum of History & Industry, Seattle.

not a forum for his storytelling; nor did he join Norwegian organizations such as the Leif Eriksson Lodge in Seattle. Rather he sought out storytelling venues among his fellow fishermen at the Fisherman's Wharf north of downtown Seattle, or in the lounges and offices of the Deep-Sea Fishermen's Union. The remarkable thing about Simonsen's stories is that they consistently portray events that took place during the first two decades of the last century; that is, during the time when he started fishing as a sixteen-year old boy in Lofoten from where he emigrated in 1908 to the Pacific Northwest, and then continued fishing at the Columbia River and in Alaska. In both instances he relied on open two-man dories when they were still legal, and life and work at sea were even more demanding and dangerous than they are now, and tested the mettle of an individual that much more. The process of self-discovery through hardships and risks taken in youth later became the yardstick by which the mature storyteller measured himself and his peers; his stories embodied what it meant to be a traditional Norwegian fisherman. Simonsen's stories are first-person narratives based upon real incidents in the life of the storyteller.[39] The style of his stories is also remarkable, recalling the terse indirectness and understatement of Norwegian folk narratives, dramatic and action-centered rather than descriptive.[40] I was able to record a baker's dozen of his stories, probably only a fraction of his repertoire, in the spring of 1990, a couple of months before he died, almost one hundred years old. Here is a sample:

Fishing at Røst

After I got over that incident, I got back to my own home near Bodø, Kjerringø. So, I shipped with a neighbor of mine. He had, it wasn't a schooner but a big sailboat, that's all they had in them days. And we took off for Røst. That's the very end of Lofoten.

And we were halfways out in the North Sea, in three days we couldn't see the islands of Lofoten. And there a storm blew up, this in January, you know. There are winter storms there, in the wintertime.

And my partner and I was in a dory, haulin' the lines back.

The lines was full of fish, they keep the gear afloat, you know.

Well, we got a heavy sea, and the dory flew right upside down, and we were in the water, both of us. Frank was his name.

Last I remember, we were working ourselves to death. He got his hand stickin' up out of the water, he said good-bye or somethin'. He went down, and never showed up no more.

Well, I was swimmin', and washed off the dory twice, nothin' to hold on to. And I didn't see that schooner of ours, couldn't see it. He lost track of the dory. We were upside down in the water.

Well, I was in the dory, and on the dory, whatever — I remember once, I was drownin' alright, because the water was all dark, when I was down there.

Dark — and I started to work back. Swim — swim the best I could, had kicked off my boots a long time ago.

And the air got lighter — lighter — lighter — lighter. And finally I got to the surface.

Well, I didn't see no boat. The boat that I belonged to. Hung on the best I could, went down again.

But I remember sometimes afterwards, that somethin' was sailin' over me, and there was a boat, that I was supposed to be in. He'd gotten washed overboard too. The boom had knocked 'im overboard, but he hung on to what we call the sheets, and got back on deck again.

And then he saw that dory, but nobody on it — But finally he saw me in the water. He saw me kickin', then he sailed right over me.

So I came up again. I was pretty well over 'n out by that time, and he managed to pick me up. My partner was drowned, of course.

Well, they claimed it took three hours to sail for shore, but, he said, I was unconscious in the foc'sle. Couldn't see any life in me.

But when I came to, he said, I bit 'im and kicked 'im, tried to poke his eyes out and everthing else, fightin' for my life.

And finally I got into Røst, where I belonged. Of course, we were through, 'cause we had lost the boat, my partner, and everything else.[41]

Chronicats: Another narrative genre alive in Norwegian American tradition in the Pacific Northwest comprises what folklorists call chronicats, that is, stories about personal experience that are not told in the first person, but about someone else whose experience is memorable enough to be recalled by a group.[42] Thus, while there are no doubt stories about U.S. Senator Henry "Scoop" Jackson (1912-1983) born in Everett, Washington to Norwegian immigrants, or about University of Washington President Charles Odegaard (1911-1999), descended from Norwegian immigrants who came to the U.S. in the 1880s, both of them men who are rightly remembered for their important contributions to the public good — to my knowledge there are no chronicats about them circulating among Norwegian Americans. Why? Because chronicats memorialize "unheard of" events identified with persons whose reputation for good or bad makes them extraordinary.

A striking example of chronicats can be found in stories told about Norwegian immigrant, sea captain Rolf Neslund whose wife murdered him in 1980, presumably because she discovered that he had another "wife" in Seattle with whom he had fathered several children. The story of Neslund made the papers from the Seattle Times to the New York Times, was bandied about on blogs for a number of years, and became the subject of "The Sea Captain," included in Ann Rule's 432-page tome *No Regrets and Other True Cases,* vol. 11, (published by Simon & Schuster in 2006) and in Rod Englert's *Blood Secrets: Chronicles of a Crime Scene Reconstructionist* (published by Barnes and Noble in 2010).

The publisher's summary describes "The Sea Captain" as follows:

A ship's pilot legendary for guiding mammoth freighters through the narrows of Puget Sound, Rolf Neslund was a proud Norwegian, a ladies' man, and a beloved resident of Washington State's idyllic Lopez Island. Virtually indestructible even into his golden years, he made electrifying headlines more than once: after a ship he was helming crashed into the soaring West Seattle Bridge, causing millions in damages; and following his inexplicable disappearance at age 80. Was he a suicide, a man broken by one costly misstep? Had he run off with a lifelong love? Or did a trail of gruesome evidence lead to the home Rolf shared with his wife, Ruth? On an island where everyone thought they knew their neighbors, the veneer of Neslund's marriage masked a convoluted case that took many years to solve. And, indeed, some still believe that the old sea captain will come home one day. "The Sea Captain" is a classic tale as blood chilling as murder itself. Along with six other equally riveting, detailed accounts of destruction and murder committed without conscience or regret, Ann Rule takes readers into frightening places they never could have imagined in *No Regrets*.

If this narrative was conveyed in oral tradition rather than in print, it would be considered a chronicat. And such chronicats about Rolf Neslund exist, albeit mostly in legendary variants told on Lopez Island, and mostly having to do with the question of what happened to Rolf's body, which was never found, or whether he would ever return. One such variant claims that Ruth showed up at Camp Norwester on Sperry Peninsula, and offered the camp several boxes of ground meat packed in plastic bags, and this offering was gratefully received by the perpetually hungry young campers. A fire fighter and first responder to the case, told me that Ruth and Rolf had in fact done their own butchering in the past, and thus Ruth was well equipped to do what the story suggested. Another variant tells that someone on the island printed a t-shirt showing an arm and hand sticking out of a burn barrel, and the caption read: "Say hello to Rolf!"[43] Shades of *Fargo* (1996)? This black comedy thriller was supposedly based on an actual criminal event, and by some audiences was understood as a riff on Norwegian American mentalities in Minnesota. Legends surrounding the possible return of Rolf, alluded to in the publisher's summary of Ann Rule's crime fiction, rehearse ancient literary models such as the 8th-century *Odyssey,* the oldest extant work of Western fiction that has inspired countless operas, films, literary works, comic strips and story cycles such as Sinbad the Sailor — and perhaps even the legendary stories about Rolf Neslund's returning to Lopez Island. The story's link to Norwegian ethnicity rests on certain putative traits of Rolf's character, whom the publisher calls a "proud Norwegian:" a muscular love of the sea, adventure, drink, women, risk taking and indestructibility, combined with a Viking propensity to go berserk. In Norse tradition, the

Berserkir, helmet plate, ca. 570-790 A.D.

berserkir (warriors wearing the "bear shirt") were known to put themselves into a fighting frenzy by ingesting certain mushrooms.[44] The Neslunds achieved the same effect through alcohol; their domestic brawls which ended in the killing of Rolf are legendary.

Memorats & fabulats: I would like to reference two other stories which, while they fall outside the current framework of narrative traditions in the Norwegian American community today, yet are connected with it. The first, the "Bear Story," is technically what folklorists call a *memorat,* that is a personal narrative about socially accepted supranormal experiences. The narrator of the story is a former student who came to our farm several times as part of an annual college class from Huxley College of the Environment in Bellingham, and we became very fond of him because of his strength of body and mind and his quick understanding of what we were trying to teach about farm sustainability and resilience. Several years ago, after he graduated, this young man suddenly called us early one morning, and this is what he told us:

I'd been hiking in the Olympic Mountains for about a week, and for the last couple of days a large bear had been following me, and when I played my flute, he ambled off. But last night, near dawn, when I was lying asleep wrapped in a tarp, the bear came back. Petrified I lay quite still and he sniffed me from head to toe and then he ambled off again. As soon as the bear had left, I jumped up, and the thought came into my mind: "I have to call Henning," but I had no idea why. I had to walk about ten miles out of the mountains before I could get any reception on my phone, but here I am, "and now please tell my why I had to call you." Henning invited me to come to Lopez Island, and I got in my truck and late the same night I arrived on the farm, where I slept in the truck, woke up, took a shower, ate breakfast with Henning and Elizabeth, and then repeated my question, "Why am I here?"

Henning explained that some days before he had been at a party on a neighboring island and there met my aunt, and they talked about me. Henning, who had just undergone eye surgery and was under strict orders not to lift anything above his head, thought to himself: "How I wish Kenny would come to the farm now, because how else am I going to bring in the barley stacked in shocks in the field to dry? And here you are!"

I was puzzled, but Henning explained that in Norwegian folk belief from the time before industrialization people knew that their thoughts could travel long distances to reach folks they were thinking about, and that often these thoughts would manifest in an animal shape reflecting the character of the sender.[45] So, the bear who came to wake me up and send me on my way must have been Henning's wishing for my help. And so we got the barley in the barn before it rained.[46]

The last story I want to mention was told to me recently by a former student, born in northern Norway who, after graduating from the University with a graduate degree in Scandinavian studies, taught Norwegian at local colleges and became a storyteller, telling the Icelandic sagas she learned about at the university, but also stories she remembered from her own childhood. One of these narratives was originally a *memorat* describing the personal experience of her great-grandmother's painful encounter with the guardian spirit of her homestead, whom she had treated disrespectfully and who beat her up in return:

My great-grandmother was born in northern Norway where the sun shines on most days during the summers, but sometimes is hidden in the mornings by clouds. So one morning, when she was doing her milking, she put her milk buckets outside her kitchen door to dry. But during the night a *hulder* came to her and said: "You mustn't do that because when you do, you hurt my child who sleeps below." So when my great-grandmother woke up the next day, she thought, "Oh, that was just a dream." So, the next morning, the sun was shining again and she dried her milk buckets outside. And sure enough, during the night the *hulder* came for the second time, and said: "I am giving you a warning. Don't dry your milk buckets in front of your kitchen door because you're hurting my child sleeping below." And then she left. So when my great-grandmother woke up, she thought: "Oh, could it be dream, or could it actually be a *hulder?*" And the third night the *hulder* came back and she brought her child with her, and it was black and blue all over, and she said: "Look at him. You did this to him, and now you deserve a beating," and she went over to my great-grandmother and gave her a beating she would never forget. And when she woke up in the morning, she was black and blue all over her entire body, and she never tried to dry her milk buckets outside her kitchen again.[47]

According to Norwegian folk belief, a *hulder* was one of the "invisible" folk, that is, a preternatural being living in close proximity with the human community.[48] They would occasionally take on human-like shape when they needed to communicate with their human neighbors. As the story makes clear, the health and well-being of both communities depended on mutual respect, and if certain boundaries were ignored, punishment would follow. Like the "Bear Story," this narrative originated as a memorat, as a story based on personal experience describing an encounter with a preternatural being. As Finnish folklorist Lauri Honko would point out, the practical function of such memorats was to enforce certain social codes,[49] in this case to correct a norm violation of an accepted interdiction against drying the milk buckets outside the kitchen door. But in the context of the Norwegian storyteller performing the story before American audiences "all over Puget Sound," the story no longer functions as a memorat because the framework of shared belief and world view, as well as familiarity with the requirements of sanitary milking protocols, is no longer given. Instead, the story functions to entertain; it becomes a *fabulat,* a fiction that fascinates modern audiences by cultural references to the past, and by its stylized form of narration. What was belief for a pre-modern culture, becomes a fiction in the modern world. Indirectly, however, such a story, even though its background in folk belief is no longer understood, serves to create a sense of identity and enculturation. In this case it serves to convey a feeling for Norwegian ethnicity.[50]

Material Culture

Dancing and Instrumental Music

Some of the liveliest traditions in the Norwegian American community in the Pacific Northwest today involve dancing, the performance of fiddle and other music, and singing. Cashion has described such performances as ritual movements or kinesiological folklore, because, unlike strictly oral traditions, their performance involves muscular activity of the whole body.[51] Remarkably, their popularity seems to be on the increase not only among Norwegian Americans, but also in the larger community, presumably because in modern consumer culture opportunities for participation in folk music and dance are not as readily available as they were even a generation ago.

Nordiska (Nordic) Folk Dancers, for example, for more than seventy-five years has provided public performances as the exhibition branch of Skandia Folk Dance Club (later Scandia Folk Dance Society), founded in 1946 by Gordon Ekvall Tracie (1920-1988). Tracie (himself of Scottish, Irish and Swedish descent) was an unflagging enthusiast for Nordic folk culture, whose classes and public festivals inspired thousands of people in the Pacific Northwest. I remember him as an exacting teacher of authentic dance traditions, painstakingly instructing the so-called *gammeldanser* (old

Nordiska Folk Dancers, Seattle, 2020. *Nordiska Weekly*.

dances) of Scandinavia which originally had migrated north from the Continent, such as the *Schottis* (from Bohemia) which in Norway is often identified with the *Reinlender* (from the Rhineland); the *Hambo* (from Hamburg); the *Pols* and *Mazurka* (from Poland); and the *Vals* (from Germany and Austria), all of them couple dances in triple meter alternating between elaborate promenades and gestures and clockwise and counter-clockwise turns. He also taught the much more difficult *bygdedanser* (village dances) such as the *springar* (roundel), a couple dance in 3/4 time native to Norway that evolved primarily in the rural communities in the western fjord areas of central Norway, together with the development of the *hardingfele* (Hardanger fiddle) in the middle of the 17th century, a special violin fitted with five resonating strings mounted below the four conventional strings to produce a distinctive droning sound. The *springar* is usually accompanied by the Hardanger fiddle — though in some communities, in Telemark, for example, the flat fiddle is also used — playing tunes composed of measures with very asymmetrical triple time beats to form traditional patterns that are rather difficult to learn. The dance is thus much freer in form than most *bygdedanser,* and was traditionally led by the male who improvised spontaneous sequences of traditional moves in response to the fiddle music and to the audience in dynamic *samspel* (interplay). There are almost as many springar and gangar traditions as there are valleys and fjords in Norway. As with the creation of the regional *bunad,* creation of a local dance is celebrated as a cultural affirmation of sorts.

In tradition, the *springar* often alternates with the *halling* (dance from Hallingdal), an acrobatic, athletic dance in 6/8 or 2/4 rhythm (96-105 beats per minute), requiring great strength and flexibility, traditionally performed by the male who would move to the center of the floor, while his female partner continued walking at the edge. Like the *springar,* the *halling* was always accompanied by fiddle music; in fact, it is the fiddler who provides the rhythmic impetus to the dancer to perform various challenging moves such as *kruking* (crossing the feet in a crouch), *hodestift* (somersault), *nakkespretten* (neck jump), and especially the *kast,* a move for which a girl holds a hat on a stick as high as six feet and the dancer kicks down the hat. During the last thirty years, the *halling* is also being performed by female dancers.

The historical context of this dance tradition makes it clear that, in Norway at least, both the music and the dancing were long considered culturally ambiguous. The Lutheran Church and especially pietistic communities like the Haugeans, saw the *halling* as sexually seductive male posturing; they regarded the music egging on the dancers as demonic and morally disruptive, and until the 20th century playing a Hardanger fiddle inside a church was forbidden.[52]

In traditional Norwegian folk belief, the Hardingfele was associated with the devil or with nature beings, specifically the *fossegrim* (spirit of the waterfall), and the best players were said to have been taught by either of those demons.[53] According to legend, one of the most famous Norwegian dance tunes, *Fanitullen* (The Devil's Tune) depicts a violent and bloody wedding that took place on a farm at Hol in Hallingdal in 1724. While the fiddler eggs on the dancers to dance whether they want to or not, one of the wedding guests spies the Devil sitting on a barrel of beer playing this tune on his own fiddle. This legend echoes the emotional effect of the sympathetic strings creating a sound as if there were a second fiddler hidden inside the fiddle. No wonder that during the religious revivals in the 1800s numerous fiddles were destroyed because people regarded the instrument and the music, as sinful encouragement of wild dances, drinking and fights.[54]

Halfdan Egedius 1877-1899, "Play & Dance," 1896.

This cultural ambiguity was poignantly illustrated by Norway's greatest mid-nineteenth century writer, Bjørnstjerne Bjørnson, in one of his incomparable novels of rural life, *Arne*, published in 1859. In the scene quoted here, describing the dancing at a wedding, we see the dynamic interaction between a social misfit, *Nils skredder* (Nils the Tailor), a drunk, notorious fighter and seducer, but also the best fiddler and dancer in the village, and the role of the community in egging on officially censured behaviors:

> Then it happened that two American tourists were in the village and heard that there was a wedding in the neighborhood and right away they wanted to come and see the local customs. Nils was playing. They each offered a dollar for playing money and asked for a *halling*. No one wanted to do it, however much they asked. Everybody said Nils should do it: "He was the best, after all." He refused all the more, the more urgent their request, until finally they all begged him with one voice, and that's what he wanted. He handed the fiddle to someone else, took off his coat and hat, stepped into the circle and smiled. Now their attention was on him again, and that gave him his

old strength. People pushed together as much as they could, those in the back crawled up on tables and benches, some girls stood way over the others, and the one in the very front — a tall girl with light brown hair, deep-set blue eyes under a high forehead, her wide mouth smiling easily and a little to one side — that was Birgit Bøen. Nils saw her as he looked up at the hat high on the stick. The music started, the crowd fell silent, and he took off. In rhythm with the fiddle he threw himself along the floor, moved to one side half aslant, cantered, crouched down and threw his legs across each other, jumped up again, stood still as if to leap — and then continued aslant again. The fiddle was in able hands. The tune took more and more fire. Nils bent his head back more and more — and all of a sudden his heel struck the hat so that the dust flew around them. They laughed and shrieked, the girls stood as if they couldn't breathe. The tune howled and egged him on to wilder and wilder jerks. And he didn't resist, leaned his body forward, took leaps in rhythm, raised himself up as if to jump, teased, cantered as before, and when it looked as if he weren't thinking about jumping at all, thundered his heel against the hat, again and again, did somersaults forwards and backwards, and then stood steady again on his feet. Then suddenly he didn't want to do it any more. The fiddle did some boisterous runs away from the tune, worked down to a deep drone, trembled away and ended with a long stroke on the bass. People spread out, talking loudly, shouts and shrieks breaking the silence. Nils stood against the wall; then the Americans came up to him and each gave him five dollars. Silence again… Nils had put one arm on the shoulder of a man standing next to him, and he was trembling so hard the man wanted to ease him down on a bench.

"Oh, it's nothing," answered Nils, took a few fumbling steps across the floor, then firmer steps, turned and asked for a *springdans*.

All the girls had come forward. He looked around, long and slow, then went straight to one in a dark dress, and that was Birgit Bøen. He reached out his hand, and she gave him both of hers; then he laughed, moved back, took the one next to her and danced wildly away. The blood shot up on Birgit's neck and in her face. A tall man with a kind face stood right behind her; he took her by the hand and danced away

— after Nils. Nils saw that, and perhaps from carelessness he danced so hard against them that the man and Birgit fell down with a crash. Laughter and shouts rose up around them. Birgit finally got up, walked aside and wept much.[55]

No doubt some of these ambivalent attitudes toward music and dancing were carried by Norwegian immigrants to America, but with the gradual secularization of society both in Norway and the U.S.,[56] that attitude has largely faded away, and today Norwegian dancing and music are considered a source of unquestioned ethnic pride. It is an indication of this shift that the preferred fiddle strings used on Hardanger fiddles in America today are imported from Norway under the name of *Fanitullen*.[57] Apparently they are of devilishly high quality.

Another traditional dance form, the so-called *turdanser* (figure dances) or *songdanser* (song dances), are associated in the Pacific Northwest with groups such as *Leikarringen* (The Dance Ring) of Leif Erikson Lodge in Seattle founded in 1970, and The Poulsbo *Leikarringen* on the Kitsap Peninsula, west of

Seattle *Leikarringen* dancing in the streets of Ballard, 2018.

Seattle. Historically, the song dance tradition was re-introduced in Norway, where it had died out after the Middle Ages, by Hulda Garborg (1862-1934), who had found the tradition intact on the Faroe Islands, although there the tradition was and remains today focused on the performance of the long medieval heroic and historical ballads.[58] She established the first *Leikarring* in Norway in 1903, with a large scale showing of *songdanser* (song dances) at the Bygdøy Folk Museum in Oslo, the same year. Today there are hundreds of song dance chapters in Norway and thousands of active members, many of them in youth groups. The dances are based on folk songs, some of medieval origin, but also on more recent folk songs such as the one about the ever popular *Per Spelman* (Fiddler Per), who traded his cow for a fiddle. The song dance is usually performed in a circle, with all the dancers singing, and the whole circle gradually moving clockwise in traditional moves referred to as *færøysteg* (Faroe Step), *folkevisesteg* (Folk Ballad Step), *kvilesteg* (Rest Step), or *attersteg* (Reverse Step). If there is a refrain in the song, it is usually formed as a "bridge," that is, a change in step, or by introducing a figure or style element from other dance forms such as the instrumental village dances or round dances. The repertoire of the Seattle *Leikarring* today includes all kinds of traditional Norwegian folk dances, from *gammeldanser* (old time dances) to *turdanser* (figure dances), to *bygdedanser* (village dances), and *sangdanser* (song dances), variously performed to musical accompaniment by flat fiddle, *hardingfele,* recorder, accordion, and occasionally the Swedish *nyckelharpa* (keyed fiddle) and *cittra* (dulcimer).

Another dance and music group to be foregrounded here, is *Lilla Spelmanslag* (Little Fiddlers' Association), a performance group of young musicians of any ethnic background, age eight to eighteen, who play dance and listening tunes from Scandinavia with the stated goal of practicing "poise, confidence and presence, while building musicianship, teamwork and leadership."[59] The group practices twice monthly, learning the music by ear, without written notes. Past performances have taken *Lilla Spelmanslag* to various venues in the Pacific Northwest, as well as to Scandinavia.

Seattle *Lilla Spelmanslag*, Seattle 2020.

Participation levels and membership in these and similar groups in the Pacific Northwest are fluid and difficult to assess numerically. Seattle *Leikarringen*, for example, does not require membership fees or charge for their practice meetings or public events. The group is supported by a grant from Leif Erikson Lodge, income from a single family donor, and by modest incomes from demonstration performances at public dance events or entertainment at retirement homes and other venues. Poulsbo *Leikarringen*, the largest Norwegian American dance organization in the Pacific Northwest, by contrast, which describes itself as a non-profit membership organization whose mission is to provide folk dance instruction that promotes and preserves Scandinavian culture and heritage, charges membership fees and offers regularly scheduled, nearly year-round classes (4:30-7pm daily) for children and youth, for pre-paid tuition. Skandia Folk Dance Society is also a member organization, although many events are open to members and non-members alike. Member benefits include reduced prices at dances and classes, and a monthly newsletter. *Lilla Spelmanslaget* requires a year-long commitment and charges a fixed annual participation fee, with allowances made for second or more children per family.

Besides these and other organizations like them, there are college-sponsored workshops, as well as numerous professional or semi-professional groups and individuals providing Scandinavian dance and music performances for the public and as tourist activities. For instance, Pacific Lutheran University in Tacoma annually sponsors workshops that typically include instruction on Norwegian folk dance, Hardanger and Norwegian flat fiddle, traditional ballad and *kvad* (poem) singing, and *bunad* (traditional Norwegian costume) construction. A partial list of noted performers of the Norwegian musical heritage in the Pacific Northwest include fiddle players Elizabeth Foster (who leads various music groups in the Seattle area); Bill Boyd (who began playing the *Hardingfele* in 1983, learning from Ingulv Eldegård, whom he succeeded as *Leikarringen's* lead musician, and who also plays with "Hale Bill & the Bops," a Scandinavian ensemble based in Tacoma)[60]; Deb Collins (a professional violin, flat and Hardanger fiddle player who performs at Norwegian heritage events and holds Hardanger fiddle workshops); Martha Levenson (the director of *Lilla Spelmanslag*); Rachel Nesvig (who plays with TinnFelen Hardanger Fiddle Ensemble); Leslie Foley (also a member of "Hale Bill & the Bops"); harp player Beth Sankey Kollé (who has taught Nordic folk dance and music on the lever harp, flute, *kvad* (poem) and Norse ballad singing for years, and has led harp concert tours to Scandinavia); accordion player Jane Anderson (a self-taught musician who began playing Nordic music in her 40s); Phil Wilkinson and Marissa Essad, co-managers of TinnFelen Hardanger Fiddle Ensemble which, besides Hardanger fiddles, includes woodwinds (flute, clarinet, oboe d'amore) and rhythm (guitar, bass); and *halling* dancer Erik Rudd (who performs at Nordic events throughout the Pacific Northwest).

The Hardanger Fiddle

The many individuals and groups performing Norwegian folk music in the Pacific Northwest today wouldn't be able to do so without access to quality instruments. Of all the folk instruments used in performing Norwegian dances, the Hardanger fiddle is the most revered.

Emile Indrebo, Tacoma. Photo by Phyllis A. Harrison.

The first known maker of Hardanger fiddles in our area was Emile Indrebo who, like his wife Solveig, emigrated from Norway and came to the Seattle area in the 1920s. After working as a logger in Washington for a lifetime, over the sixteen years between retirement in 1972 and his death in 1988, he built forty-two Hardanger fiddles, most of them finding their way into the hands of musicians in the local Scandinavian community.[61] He had learned the art of fiddle making at age twelve from a teacher in Norway and carried it to the New World. Another fiddle maker currently active in the Pacific Northwest is Lynn Berg, born in North Dakota, the grandson of Norwegian immigrants on both sides of his family, who moved to Eugene, Oregon nearly three decades ago. He learned to make fiddles through an academic program at the University of New Hampshire and subsequently honed his skills by seeking out a master fiddle maker in Norway. Making violins since 1993, he has since built one hundred twenty-nine instruments, most of them Hardanger fiddles, and all but two of them remain in the Pacific Northwest today.[62]

The Hardanger fiddle originated in southwestern Norway, where it is still used for dancing, accompanied by rhythmic loud foot stomping. It was also traditional for the fiddler to lead the bridal procession to the church. The earliest known Hardanger fiddle was made in 1651 by a farmer by the name of Ole

Jonsen Jaastad. It had a round, narrow body, but by 1850 a body much like that of a modern violin had come into use. About 100 years after Jaastad, a father and son team of luthiers from the Hardanger region sold more than a thousand Hardanger fiddles all over Norway. The father, Isak Nilsen Botnen (1669-1759), was a professional instrument maker often considered the Stradivarius of the Norwegian fiddle; his son, Trond Isaksen Flatebø (1713–1772), experimented widely with the design of the instrument. Their influence in all probability shaped the quality and popularity of fiddle music in Norway and helped eclipse other folk instruments such as the flute, *langeleik* (zither played with one top string and several resonating under strings), or the folk harp.

The defining characteristic of the Hardanger fiddle is that it has eight or nine strings, of which the top four are strung and played like a flat violin, while the four or five under strings resonate to the top four. The instrument is often highly decorated with the mythological dragon known, for example, from Norway's medieval stave churches, or the emblematic lion of Norway's royal house, or the head of a woman, and embellished with mother of pearl inlay and decorations in black ink referred to as *rosing,* a form of rose painting that developed in the 18th century from baroque and rococo models as decorations on walls, ceilings and furniture in the rural valleys of Norway.[63] Lynn Berg also developed analog versions for the viola and cello to provide instruments for the Harding Quartet, which premiered in 2002 in Tacoma featuring arrangements of traditional fiddle tunes and original compositions in the style of Norwegian folk music.

Harding Quartet

The Hardanger fiddle is a so-called transposing instrument which means that music for it is written in a different key than the one heard when the instrument plays the music. For example, since the *Hardingfele* is a D instrument, music written for it will be in C corresponding to D on a non-transposing instrument like the piano. The most common tuning for the top strings of a Hardanger fiddle is A-D-A-E, with the under strings vibrating B-D-E-F♯-A; however, specific tuning mostly depends on the tradition area the tune comes from, and more than twenty different tunings have been recorded in Norway. The famous *Fanitullen* (Devil's Tune) requires the fiddle to be "troll-tuned" (A-E-A-C♯) for greatest emotional effect. In the Valdres district of Norway, this particular tuning is called *grålysning* ("grey-lighting," meaning day-break), implying that the fiddler tuned his fiddle like this after he had played through the night, and his audience was now ready to go over the edge. A compelling modern version of the tune, "Fanitullen Goes to America," was released in 2004 by *Bukkene Bruse* ("Three Billy Goats Gruff"), a Norwegian musical group that fuses Norwegian folk songs with other musical traditions.

Choral Singing

Norwegian American traditions of choral singing are mostly associated with the numerous local performance groups organized as part of the Norwegian Singers Association of America in Illinois, Iowa, Minnesota, South Dakota, and Wisconsin (eleven choruses) and, on the West Coast, as the Pacific Coast Norwegian Singers Association (twelve choruses located in California, Oregon, and Washington).[64] Unlike the fraternal organizations, for instance the "Sons of Norway" established in America in 1895 by Norwegian immigrants as mutual aid societies patterned on community models in pre-industrial Norway,[65] the twenty-three choral groups now in existence are all descended from a specific singers' organization in Norway. This organization, *Den Norske Studentsangforening* (The Norwegian Students' Singing Society), was Norway's first male chorus, organized by Johan Didrik Behrens in 1845 in Bergen. In June 1851, the first *Sangerfest* (singers' festival) was held in Asker, Norway. Five years later the first immigrant male chorus was organized in America and, by 1886, enough choruses had been established to form a *Sangerforbund* (Singers Association). On the West Coast, the first chorus was organized in Portland, Oregon, in 1878, and by 1902, the "Pacific Coast Norwegian Singers Association" was established in Seattle. The Norwegian American choruses followed the example of the Norwegian Students' Singing Society by celebrating annual singers' festivals, the first one being hosted by the

Everett Norwegian Male Chorus formed in 1903, and repeated most years since then. In 1981, the Pacific Coast Norwegian Singers Association took one hundred Norwegian American singers and their families and friends on a concert tour to Norway, followed by several performance tours between 1990 and 1997. In turn, choruses from Norway joined in annual singers' festivals in America.

The membership of these choruses was exclusively male, and they focused on public performances. Their current repertoire of forty-six titles reproduces that of their Norwegian model, and consists mostly of 19th century patriotic and Romantic songs by Norwegian poets Henrik Anker Bjerregaard (1792-1842), Johan Sebastian Welhaven (1809-1883), Henrik Wergeland (1808-1845), Ivar Aasen (1813-1896), Andreas Munch (1811-1884), Bjørnstjerne Bjørnson (1832-1910), Per Sivle (1857-1904), Arne Garborg (1851-1924), Theodor Caspari (1853-1948), hymn writer Elias Blix (1869-1891) plus a number of minor writers, as well as Swedish poets Carl Michael Bellman (1740-1795), Gustav Fröding (1860-1911), Erik Gustaf Geijer (1783-1847) and Swedish-Finnish Johan Ludvig Runeberg (1804-1877). The songs were mostly set to music by lesser known German, Danish and Swedish composers. Later in the century, however, major Norwegian composers, Rikard Nordraak (1842-1866), Halvdan Kjerulf (1815-1868), and Edvard Grieg (1843-1907) contributed unforgettable melodies to the repertoire, among them Nordraak's setting to Norway's national anthem, "Ja vi esker dette landet" (Yes, We Love This Land) by Bjørnson, as well as Grieg's musical interpretation of Bjørnson's "Landkjenning" (Land Sighting), a nationalist poem based on the saga hero Olav Tryggvason, appropriate before Norway regained its full independence as a country in 1905. Norwegian American Alfred Paulsen (1849-1936) provided the melody to Conradi's patriotic song *Norge, mitt Norge* (Norway, my Norway). The remainder of the repertoire includes a couple of sea shanties, several songs based on folk belief and folk life, and descriptions of the ocean, fjords, and mountains. All of the songs in the repertoire were translated by Alf Lunder Knudsen (who wrote a doctoral dissertation on the history of Norwegian choral groups in the U.S.), because most of the singers do not know the language any more and depend on translations. Besides the annual singers' festivals, the choral groups perform at cross-cultural festivals such as Northwest Folklife in Seattle, and at retirement homes and other venues.

The history of Norwegian American women's choral groups differs markedly from that of the men's. It is closely tied to the Daughters of Norway of the Pacific Coast founded 1908 as a mutual aid society for women immigrants, much like the Sons of Norway, with forty-four lodges established between 1905-2002 and a current membership of 1,700. It is interesting to note that the membership of the Daughters of Norway has always been much smaller than that of the Sons of Norway, which in 2013 claimed 58,000 members in 400 lodges in the United States, Canada and Norway (down from 90,000 members in 1995, and 64,186 members in 2010),[66] about 1.5% of the 4.5 million self-declared Norwegian Americans reported on the 1990 federal census.[67] The practice of singing in the context of the Daughters of Norway rarely takes the shape of performances in formal audience settings, unlike the performances by the The Norwegian Ladies Chorus of Seattle, founded in 1936 by August Werner, Norwegian-born professor of music at the University of Washington. The focus of the "Ladies Chorus" is "to study and sing Norwegian music by Norwegian composers and to perform limited selections of other appropriate music in English and various Scandinavian languages."[68] By contrast, the song practice of the Daughters of Norway emphasizes lodge meetings, programs and events. In 1923, the Daughters of Norway produced a small song book that featured seven songs written by and for members of the organization, rather than songs by Norwegian poets and composers. The book featured songs that gave musical expression to the identity of the Daughters of Norway and were intended to set various organizational rituals to music — for example, openings and closings of meetings, initiations and funeral rites for deceased members, to celebrate sisterhood among themselves, and loyalty to the Norwegian flag.[69] The 1967 edition of the song book added the American national anthem to the Norwegian, provided translations of some of the songs, and included several new titles, such as the "Daughters' Fight Song." The third edition of the song book in 2018, edited by Beth Kollé and Janet Ruud, greatly expanded the selection of songs, most of them paired with translations, and combined with notation, piano arrangements and guitar chords by Beth Kollé. The editors expressed the hope that in its new form, the book would be used not only in lodge meetings, programs and events, but would also be treasured in the personal lives of singers. The much larger repertoire of seventy-six songs now includes: National Songs and Hymns, Traditional Songs and Folk Songs, Children's Songs, Christmas Songs, Fun Songs, as well as the Daughters of Norway Songs from 1923 and

1967. Both the performance groups and the song book make valuable contributions to the preservation of Norwegian American tradition. Singing together helps maintain their sense of community as people who identify with their heritage and pass that sense on to the next generation. The men's performance groups display to the public their pride in Norwegian poetry and music, while the women's singing brings the culture into their organizations as well as into their homes, singing around the Christmas tree and at other significant family occasions. Both are examples of participatory culture rather than passive cultural consumption through the popular media.

Husflid

Many Norwegian Americans take pleasure in decorating their homes with craft items such as pewter ware, traditional clothing and jewelry, weavings, wooden implements, toys, or old pieces of furniture that came down to them from their immigrant ancestors or that they purchased in ethnic import stores at home or in Norway.[70] A minority still practice sewing, knitting, weaving, jewelry making, wood carving[71], instrument making, boat building, *rosemaling* (rose

Anders Monsen Askevold (1834–1900). Milking and knitting at the *seter* (mountain farm). N.d.

painting)[72], and such, as leisure time folk art expressions; but the connection of such products, whether homemade or purchased, to their socio-economic function in preindustrial Norway has mostly been forgotten. It is important to remember that the half million emigrants that had left Norway by 1900 for a new life in America came from farms where self-sufficiency encompassed not only food production, but also the production of most material goods required for daily life and work: clothing, housing and agricultural buildings, boats, plows and other farming implements, and wood working, smithing and other tools. In most instances farmers also produced the raw materials from which to make these goods: wool, thread and linen for sewing, weaving and knitting; dyes made from birch bark, flowers, lichens and other vegetable matter for color; wax for candles; fats for soap; skins for shoes and clothes; hemp and tree shavings for rope; wood for building houses, sleds and boats, and for crafting furniture, kitchen and other implements; charcoal and bog iron for tool making. As vital

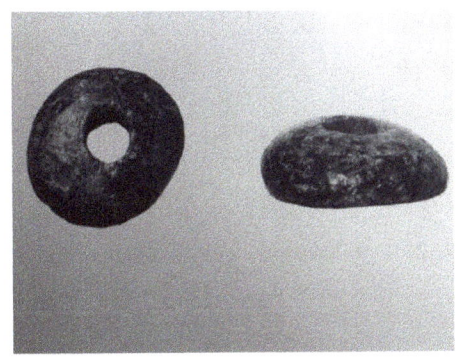

Soapstone spinning whorl from 11th-century.

Modern drop spindle improvised from an old Norwegian coin and a knitting needle (Studio Emiglia 2).

economic activities on any farm, *husflid* (home crafts) involved the whole family, both during the work day and in the evening when men, women and children would gather in the *stue* (kitchen-living room), weaving, spinning, whittling wooden tools, repairing fishing nets, and making rope, harness, knives, shoes and much more.

Often a member of the household or itinerant worker would be designated to entertain the group by telling stories or playing an instrument, or singing, rather than working.[73] Over time, the forms of these domestic products took on a regional quality, such as the *bunad* that reflects the traditional clothing styles of different regions in Norway. At times these necessary activities would rise to the level of individual artistic expression in the sense that form exceeded function: for instance, when a carver decorated a homemade bedstead with an imaginary figure, or painted roses on a chest holding grain or family heirlooms, or embellished a fishing knife with inlaid silver, or a bridal dress with lace embroidery. Sometimes the craftspeople were not members of the family but itinerant seamstresses, tailors, shoemakers, button molders, hat makers, and others, who moved from farm to farm and stayed long enough to supply the household with whatever they needed for the year; but not everyone could afford outside help, and most clothing, shoes, tools, implements, furniture, and the like was produced at home, in keeping with regional traditions in form, style and color. With the industrialization of Norway after World War I, however, the traditional rural culture of Norway changed radically in response to local and world-wide economic developments, and self-sufficiency of farms in producing not only food but also crafts in the comprehensive sense of supplying the material needs of households, became rare or survived mostly in the form of craft products sold to the general public and in the tourist market. Museums and commercial outlets became the venues for pre-industrial folk crafts. *Husfliden*, the national chain of associated folk designers, artisans, large-scale fabricators and stores, took the place of *husfliden,* the traditional home crafts that met the everyday needs of local farm households. For Norwegian Americans today, the charm of pre-industrial technologies rooted in rural culture combines with a personal longing for a level of ethnic identity not commonly offered in American culture. For a consumer used to supplying her material needs from industrial sources, a

Carding and spinning wool on a Saxon-style spinning wheel on a 19th-century farm in Telemark, Norway (Wordpress).

seemingly handmade item carries significant symbolic meanings identified with the consumer's felt ethnic background.[74]

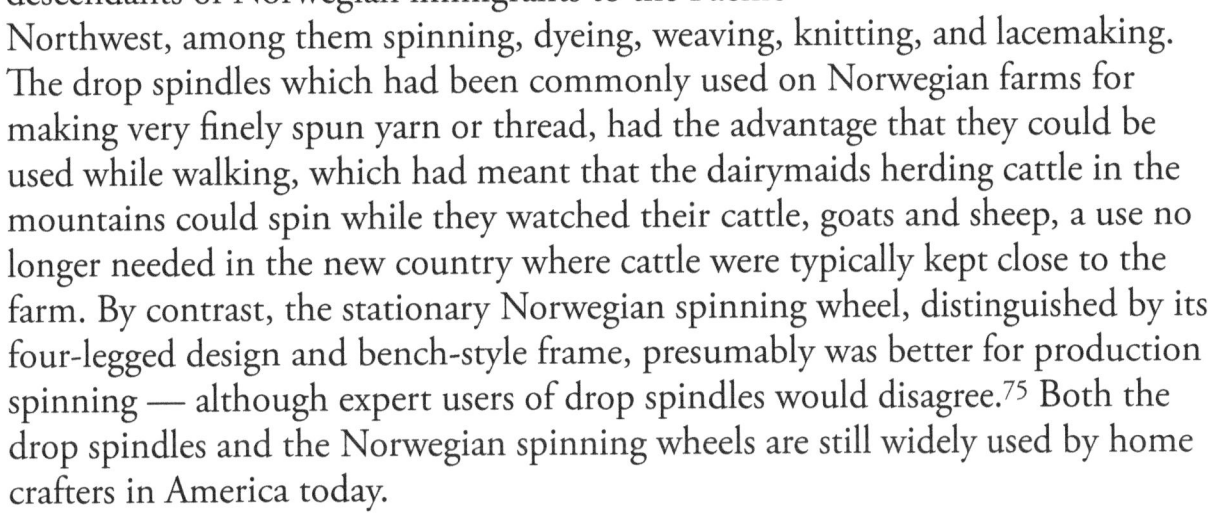

Spinning, Weaving, Knitting & Lace Making

A number of traditional *husflid* crafts, however, continue to be cultivated by the descendants of Norwegian immigrants to the Pacific Northwest, among them spinning, dyeing, weaving, knitting, and lacemaking. The drop spindles which had been commonly used on Norwegian farms for making very finely spun yarn or thread, had the advantage that they could be used while walking, which had meant that the dairymaids herding cattle in the mountains could spin while they watched their cattle, goats and sheep, a use no longer needed in the new country where cattle were typically kept close to the farm. By contrast, the stationary Norwegian spinning wheel, distinguished by its four-legged design and bench-style frame, presumably was better for production spinning — although expert users of drop spindles would disagree.[75] Both the drop spindles and the Norwegian spinning wheels are still widely used by home crafters in America today.

Until well into the 18th century, and in some outlying districts even later, the ancient vertical, warp-weighted loom of Norway, consisting of a simple upright frame with two horizontal beams, leaning against a wall,[76] was the principal tool to produce *vadmål* (cloth measure), a coarse, dense, usually un-dyed 2/2 twill weave made mostly from sheep wool and used to make the clothing for working people. Typically, *vadmål* was felted until it was thick, strong and resisted rain and wind, like the famous *Loden* cloth made by the farmers of Bavaria, Austria and Tyrol. Until factory-made fabrics became available and affordable, Norwegian immigrants continued to produce homespun fabric, but their looms were soon replaced by more efficient American floor looms that offered greater production speed and the ability to weave both longer and wider pieces of fabric and achieve greater variability in weaving pattern.

Traditional Sámi vertical tapestry loom, without warp weights, ca. 1750-1850 (Maihaugen).

Spinning & Weaving: For the most part, Norwegian American weavers no longer produce fabric for clothing, and weaving is rarely a function of home economics, although many weavers incorporate Scandinavian design in household linens. The distinction to be made is that while such items have a utilitarian function, they are not produced to meet the needs of self-sufficient households, and their attractiveness to potential buyers depends mostly on their esthetic and ethnic qualities. By and large, the focus of the craft now rests on artistic self-expression and individual creativity in the pattern. Typical weaving products include tapestries, wall hangings, floor art, coverlets, kitchen textiles, towels and runners. Many of the weaving patterns (*setts*), however, are traditional and were brought to the U.S. by immigrants and craft teachers. Traditional weaving patterns such as *krokbragd* (Bound Weave), a weft-faced weaving technique, and *rosebragd* (Rose Path), have passed into American design repertoires through the work of artists such as Linda Caspersen, a first generation Norwegian American who studied weaving in Norway, and for the last twenty years has been Textile Curator and Collections Manager at the Scandinavian Center at Pacific Lutheran University in Tacoma and has taught many courses and workshops.[77]

As Linda points out there are three basic weaving patterns that are universal: "plain weave," "twill weave," and "satin weave," and these are found the world over. Traditional Norwegian *krokbragd* is an example of twill weave because the pattern of the heddles in setting up the loom produces the diagonal line indicative of twill. *Rosebragd* is a popular variation of the basic twill weave that is easier to set up. *Tavlebragd* (Monk's Belt) is an example of plain weave using "floating" patterns to create the design. Satin weave is distinguished by the requirement to have a minimum of five harnesses, but no binding points, which is why linens made with linen thread are so fine in texture. In any traditional

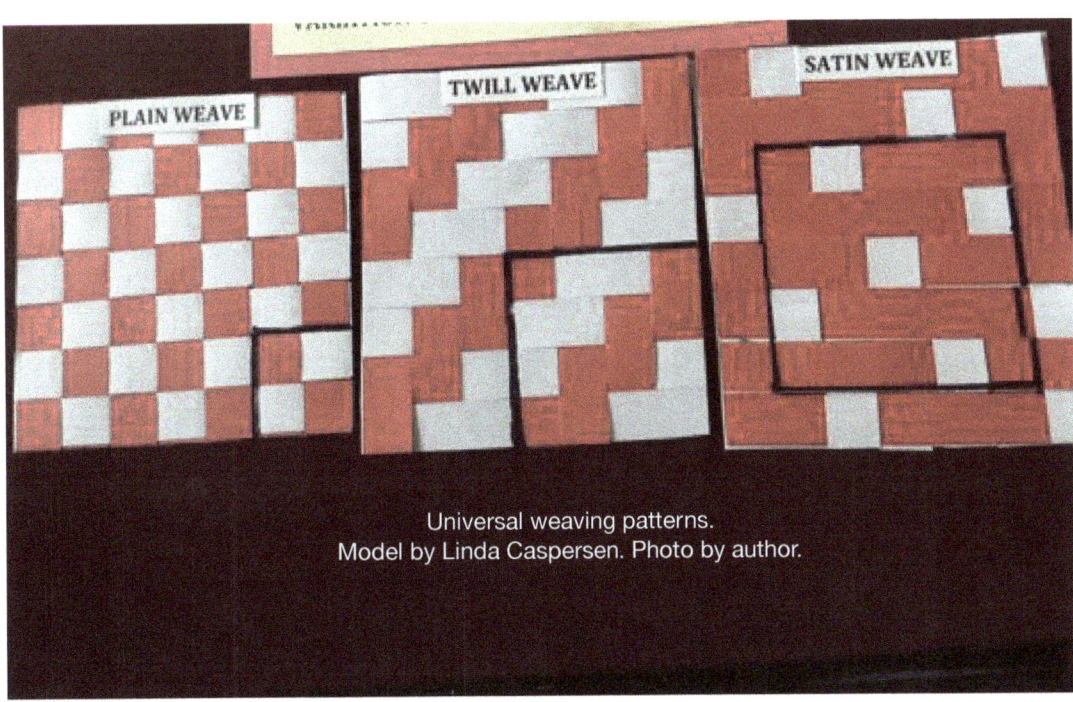

Universal weaving patterns.
Model by Linda Caspersen. Photo by author.

pattern, the distinguishing design is a function of the technique of setting up the loom to determine the points where warp and weft meet at ninety degrees to create the connection. Of course, there are other categories of textiles: knits and non-woven textiles employ a different process altogether.

Traditional *Vestlandsåkle* (coverlet from western Norway) in *krokbragd weave*.
Property of Linda Caspersen. Photo by author.

Knitting: While Norwegian American weaving traditions have mostly become a pure art form, knitting traditions have retained a strong connection to making clothing such as sweaters, socks and stockings, mittens, shawls, hats and other garments. Norwegian sweaters, among them most notably the highly decorated, colorful *Setesdal lusekofter* (Lice Sweaters), have become prized "ethnic" objects and valuable merchandise in the tourist trade. What used to be a homespun cardigan or worsted jacket formerly worn by farmers and made entirely of sheep wool, have transmuted into fashionable garments, made partly of sheep wool, but mostly from other fibers such as mohair (angora goat hair), and synthetics (acrylics and viscose), and most frequently machine-produced, e.g. by *Dale of Norway* and *Oleana,* and other industrial-scale producers supplying *Husfliden* and other tourist-based outlets. Nevertheless, knitting remains a beloved and widely practiced home craft and art form. As Beth Kollé describes it:

> There is a lot of interest in knitting Norwegian sweaters, especially *Setesdal lusekofter.* The "lice" are the little stitches of contrasting color on the lower part of the sweater which are both decorative and add another layer of wool for warmth. The upper part of the sweater has a horizontal two-color pattern, such as crossed skis, reindeer, or an 8-point star. The collar, front placket (opening at the neck or sleeve) and sometimes the cuffs are made of embroidered felted wool. The *ekte* (genuine) embroidery is called *løyesaum* (Leaf Embroidery), but today the more commonly seen embroidery is what Annemor Sundbø — a traditional textile designer and teacher in Setesdal — [78] deprecates as "cheap Oslo knock-off embroidery."

> Norwegians use the same knitting technique that many Americans do, but their approach to knitting drop-shoulder sweaters is different. Americans tend to read a pattern, knitting front left, front right and back and shaping shallow indentations where the sleeves will fit, knit both sleeves so that they are fitted into those indentations, and sew them all together. After making a number of those, some knitters can whomp out a sweater without written instructions. By contrast, Norwegians often don't use a pattern at all; after they have been knitting for some time, they simply figure it out as they go, knitting from some point around the waist or hip up to the shoulder with no shaping for sleeves, then knitting two sleeves with only a taper from wrist up to armpit. Then two long slits are cut on either side of the body and the tops of the sleeves are sewn in.

Besides sweaters in the traditional Norwegian style, knitting mittens is a popular American craft. In 2007, Terri Shea of Ballard wrote a well received

From Shea, Terri 2007. *SELBUVOTTER: Biography of a Knitting Tradition*. Spinningwheel.

book on the history of Selbu knitting which provides instructions and patterns for creating a variety of mittens and gloves,[79] and in 2011 she republished the classic volume, *Norwegian Knitting Designs*.[80] Another book on the same topic by Norwegian knitter Anne Bårdsgård, was reviewed by Beth Kollé in the *Norwegian American* (2020). Each year in October the Nordic Museum in Seattle hosts a knitting festival, and knitters and designers have come from Scandinavia to teach at the museum or set up a class at a local knit shop.

Hardangersøm by Marie Bakke Bremner
Photo by Jens Lund.

Lacemaking: Lacemaking is another Norwegian craft tradition that is alive in the Pacific Northwest. For example, Marie Bakke Bremner (1929-2013) in Republic, Washington, was renowned for her skill with a needle: embroidery, knitting, quilting, cross stitch, and traditional *Hardangersøm* (Hardanger lace) — a form of counted-thread cutwork she learned from her mother, an immigrant from the Hardanger region in Western Norway, where the development of lacework in Europe since the Renaissance had perhaps found its highest expression.[81] Beth Kollé, who is also a member of Lacemakers of Puget Sound,[82] describes her own practice of Norwegian-style lace making as follows:

4" wide bobbin lace border believed to belong to Beth Kollé's maternal great-great-grandmother, Anna Marie Fjeld (immigrated 1861). Photo by Beth Kollé.

Lace can be knitted, crocheted, tatted, embroidered — or woven, as in bobbin lace. Also called pillow lace, the threads are wound onto bobbins. It is basically off-loom weaving, with the threads secured on the pillow with pins until the project is complete and the pins can be removed. I learned bobbin lace in the 1980s and produced a good number of projects, including gold Torchon lace for Lori Talcott's Telemark-style wedding hat,[83] *bunad* silver lace for a friend in Norway, and linen lace on the baby cap for my Norwegian cousin's granddaughter.[84]

Bunad

A special place in Norwegian folk crafts is held by the *bunad* (from Old Norse *búnaðr* (outfit, dress), originally a rural garment now conventionally referred to as Norway's "national" costume, but more accurately described as "regional," because the *bunad* differs widely between tradition regions, of which more than 450 have been officially identified.[85] As a traditional garment, the *bunad* derives from the *folkedrakt* (folk attire) commonly worn by farmers in the 18th and 19th centuries, but with roots going back to the Middle Ages. The modern use of the term *bunad*, however, is a 20th-century convention, and the dresses offered today by outlets such as *Husfliden* are only loosely based on traditional work clothes.

19th-century Telemark couple, the woman in a *beltestakk* (belted skirt), the man in *vadmål* knee pants, *gråkufte* (bleached homespun jacket), knitted knee socks and felt hat. Photo by Axel Lindstad. Norsk Folkemuseum.

The fascination with peasant attire stems from 19th-century National Romanticism in Norway, as well as in Denmark and notably Germany. However in Norway, National Romantic ideas had a more lasting impact, mostly because of the pioneering work of women like Klara Semb (1884–1970) and Hulda Garborg (1862–1934), whose book *Norsk Klædebunad* (Norwegian Local Dress) published in 1903, encouraged the self-conscious development of regional

Gerhard Munthe (1849-1929), Hallingdal Woman in Work Attire, 1890.

costumes. Modern, commercial interpretations of these costumes have often done away with parts of the traditional dresses and enhanced others, in order to align them with more contemporary ideas of beauty and fashion. For instance, the headdresses and headpieces that traditionally indicated a woman's social or marital status, have given way to the modern women's fashion of showing their hair. As a recognized "national" costume, today the *bunad* has gained the status of gala attire, worn not only at folk dances, weddings, baptisms, confirmations and especially the *Syttende Mai* (Constitution Day) celebrations, but also at official occasions such as formal dinners held at the royal castle. It is a significant symbolic gesture for the royal family to appear in *bunad* at the public celebration of *Syttende Mai*, a deliberate sign of identification of Norwegian culture with that of the historical *bonde* (from Old Norse *bóndi*, literally "one who is rooted in a place"). Until the turn of the 20th century, farmers constituted more than 80% of the entire population, but nevertheless occupied a much lower rung on the social ladder than civil servants, ministers, professionals or educators, or the nobility (abolished in 1823), let alone royalty. Today a *bunad* ranks as a coveted status symbol identified with Norwegian ethnicity.

Another telling difference between Norway and Norwegian America in regard to wearing Norway's "national" costume, is so-called *bunadskikk* (dress custom) first established with Hulda Garborg, then cemented into rules by the *Landsnemda for Bunad Spørsmål* (National *Bunad* Board), a committee dedicated to the strict enforcement of formal requirements for *bunad* fabric and construction, and for accessories such as shoes, stockings, coats, capes, caps, jewelry, hair style and makeup (not allowed) — even the important question of who could wear what *bunad,* and for what use. The underlying question concerns the right of tradition communities to safeguard their own heritage.

Halfdan Egedius' famous painting of two girls dancing in a dimly lit room in Telemark richly illustrates the intimate connection between dress and cultural

Halfdan Egedius, *Dans i storstuen* (Dance in the Big Room), 1895.

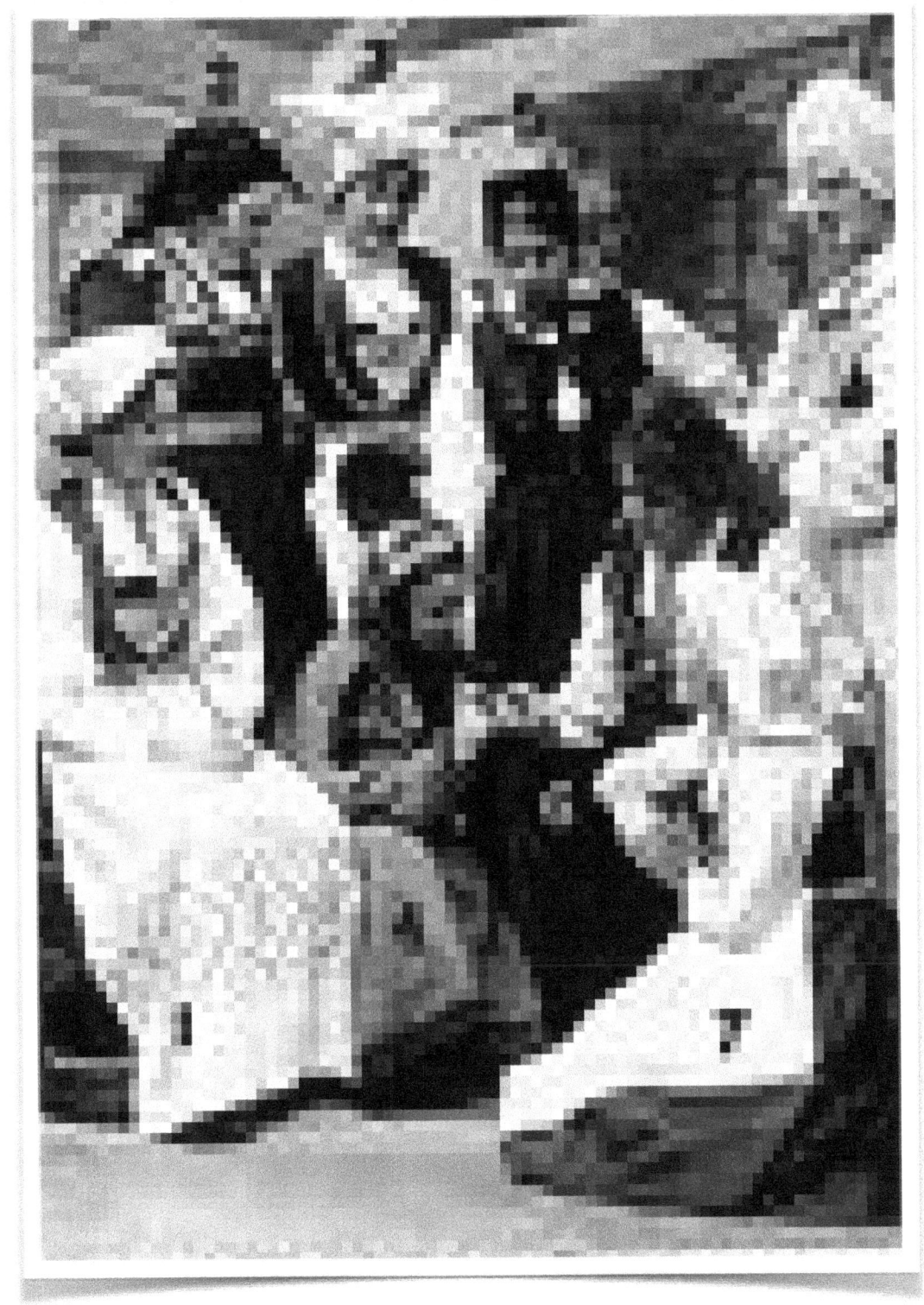

Bunad: Hardanger (1), Setesdal (2), Sogn (3), Finnmark (4), Sunnmøre (5), Hulda Garborg in Hallingdal *bunad* (6), Voss (7), Fana (8). Nasjonalbiblioteket.

practice. The rhythm of the dance movement performed by the two girls would be unthinkable without the shape and weight of their dresses. As Linda Caspersen explains:

The lower hem of the Telemark *beltestakk* is weighted with horse hair and thick wool, both cut on the bias. This helps shape the undulating 6" deep hem into a circle before attaching it to the skirt. The bottom edge of 5.5 meters has to fit into the 4.6 meters at the bottom edge of the *stakk*. Many rows of stitching and steaming with an iron help to create this shape. On the Setesdal drakt from the 1800s, it is apparent that the back of the *stakk* is quite different from the front. It appears to have a "plisse" effect. This crimping is created by hand stitching a large piece of handwoven wool to a much narrower width. This white wool is taken into the woods and boiled in an iron pot filled with tree bark in order to create the dark brown/black natural dye color. The dyed wool piece is then rolled onto a wooden drum and stored for 1 to 2 years. When removed from the drum, the hand stitching is pulled out and the crimp is permanent. It is then attached to the rest of the skirt. The bottom of this costume is also weighted like the Telemark *beltestakk*.

Once set in motion, the heavy skirt would act like a fly-wheel pulling the dancer in perpetual motion. Egedius dramatically captures this dynamic interplay of music, body rhythm and garment, and of the two dancers with the village audience surrounding them. The picture demonstrates that folk dress is more than a decorative costume: it embodies a deeply felt cultural image.

Reflecting the historical embeddedness of the production of the wool and the construction of the costumes, the *Landsnemda for Bunad Spørsmål* established rules that anyone wanting to wear a *bunad* should have family or a living cultural connection to the region of the garment. Jewelry to be worn with the dress had to be *arvesølv* (heirloom silver) or specifically created for the *bunad* in traditional style. Personally designed variations of *bunad* were not allowed, and *Husfliden* was not permitted to sell the *bunad* to tourists without the requisite connection to a regional tradition. Norwegian Americans who wanted a *bunad* pretty much had to travel to Norway and try to convince *Husfliden* to sell them one. Making your own, from American fabrics and perhaps your own design, was considered in poor taste. Only mass-produced *sølje* was generally available for purchase; hand-crafted *sølje* was nearly impossible to find in the U.S.

In the 1990s, however, the *Landsnemda* relaxed its rules. Americans especially felt that anyone who had the money should be allowed to purchase and wear a *bunad* of choice, but not everyone could afford to pay $3,000-$10,000 for a genuine one handmade by an artisan, and so many people were left out. Making your own *fantasidrakt* (Fantasy Costume) became more acceptable, and variations appeared, and even earrings were being worn. In Seattle, "fantasy costumes" can be observed at the dances arranged by the Sons of Norway, for example, where especially girls and women, but often also boys and men, wear simple dresses, shirts, skirts, knee pants and vests patterned on traditional work clothes. The girls of Seattle's *Lilla Spelmanslaget* (Little Fiddler Group), most of whom are not of Norwegian descent, go one step further. They perform their concerts of traditional Nordic string music in homemade costumes of long skirts, shirts, vests and scarves made from various colorful materials loosely reminiscent of the dress customs of the rural folk of pre-industrial Scandinavia.

Linda Caspersen with *Fantasidrakt* *(fantasy folk costume)* she made from remnants.

Nevertheless, many Norwegian Americans continue to take pride in the historicity of their ethnic background represented by a regional *bunad*. The stories of how Jody Grage and Beth Sankey Kollé, both Norwegian Americans, each came by her traditional dress exemplify this context. Jody Thorsen Grage, born in Seattle of a Norwegian sailor from Telemark who had stowed away on a Norwegian ship as a cabin boy and eventually landed in Tacoma, is one of the original Sustainable Seattle and Sustainable Ballard organizers. A retired special education teacher, she lives in the oldest house in Ballard surrounded by her vegetable garden, doing needlework, sewing Norwegian folk costumes, and practicing voluntary simplicity, peacekeeping, and community work, and teaching knitting at Sustainable Ballard Knitters for the Homeless.[86] She learned knitting from her mother and bunadsøm (*bunad* sewing) in Norway when she returned there to find her father's family in Telemark. A couple of decades ago, she made the Telemark *beltestakk* (belted skirt) for the wedding of, and under the direction of, her friend Kari-Anne Pedersen, curator of costumes and textiles at the Norwegian Folk Museum on Bygdøy and author of *Bunad og Folkedrakt: Beltestakk før og nå. Levende norske tradisjoner* (*Bunad* and Folk Attire: The Belt Skirt Then and Now. Living Norwegian Traditions).[87] After the wedding, Jody spent two more months sewing her own *beltestakk* before returning home to Seattle.

Beth Sankey Kollé, also born in Seattle, from Norwegian immigrant forebears who came to the Pacific Northwest in the 1890s from Minnesota, learned to knit *kofter* with *løyasaum* (leaf seam embroidery) from a Norwegian cousin, to knit from her grandmothers, and to embroider from Norwegian knitter Annemor Sundbø. She learned *knipling* (bobbin lace) on her own and from experimental college classes in the Seattle area. Her regional costume, a Telemark *stakk og liv* (skirt and bodice) represents a continuous tradition antedating even the categorical descriptions issued by the National Bunad Board, which means wearers are free to choose, for example, any blouse for the dress as long as it is sewn in the traditional drop-shoulder style.

Beth was in Telemark in 1986 to learn the local *springar* and *gangar* (roundel dances of varying tempos). She was able to persuade the local *Husfliden* to cut the pattern and wool fabric pieces for her, from which she assembled the gown when she returned to Seattle. The blouse was given to her by the American wife of a Norwegian friend living in Oslo. The Telemark-style *sølje:* a small brooch holding the blouse collar together, the large circular brooch at the bodice opening, the belt buckles, as well as her blouse cufflinks, were all made in Seattle by Lori Talcott, a silversmith who had learned her craft in Norway.

Lori Talcott (left) & Jody Grage, (right) each in her Telemark *beltestakk,* both wearing married women's headdresses.

Lori Talcott's own story of how she came by her *beltestakk* differs from those of Jody and Beth in that Lori is not of Norwegian descent, and her connection to the costume and jewelry traditions of Norway is that of a "humble guest," who as a silversmith has been "invited to honor the tradition" by accepting the dress representing the Telemark region where she apprenticed, did research and taught for years. The dress was sewn for her by Kari-Anne Pedersen, the same who helped Jody sew her *beltestakk.*[88] Lori makes the point that Jody's, Beth's and her own costume represent the customary folk dress worn by some elder women in Telemark until well into

Beth Sankey Kollé in her Telemark *stakk og liv*. Photo by Jack Kollé.

the 1970s. By contrast, the *bunad* self-consciously promoted as national costume by Hulda Garborg and Klara Semb at the beginning of the 20th century was ideally based on *vestlandsdrakt* (West Coast Dress), while the Telemark folk dress was less favored as putative national costume. Today, however, the *beltestakk* is recognized as part of an unbroken, ancient *bunad* tradition of farming attire, but with its own esthetic history.

Traditional *slangesølje* from Seljord, Telemark. Photo by Anne-Lise Reinsfelt, Norwegian Folk Museum.

Jewelry

The festive dresses worn in rural communities in 19th-century Norway reflect the tradition of the richest possible adornment with intricate *arvesølv* (heirloom silver) as displays of family wealth and craftsmanship. As Norwegian silversmith and folklorist Hilde Nødtvedt explains on her website,[89] the intricate *sølje* — silver gilt plates, brooches, chains and belt buckles — were traditionally handmade by artisan jewelers working independently of established craft guilds typically found in the towns of Norway. These artisans were mostly *småkårsbønder* (cotters of modest means) commissioned by richer members of their communities. Silver was expensive — the historical mines in Kongsberg in operation from 1623 until 1958 altogether produced no more than three metric tons of silver[90] — and only the well-to-do could afford to decorate their *bunad* with the precious metal. Less wealthy would typically use clothing fasteners made from other metals. However, besides the symbolic function of displaying family wealth — and the practical function of clasps, brooches, buttons or chains holding garments together — heirloom silver and anything made of metal had another and equally important function: namely as a protective talisman against intrusive nature spirits.[91] A silver penny, for example, blessed by a priest or minister and sewn onto the shirt of a newborn child, would protect it against the *usynlige* (invisible folk) believed to live at the edge of the human world.[92] Paradoxically, it was also believed that the finest jewelry was fashioned with help from the same nature spirits: it was thought to be too perfect to have been made by human hands alone. Silver was also thought to have power to heal snakebite, still a bleeding, aid beer fermentation, and increase

Traditional bridal hat from Tinn, Telemark. Reconstructed from original in Norsk Folkemuseum, Oslo, for Talcott exhibition at the Nordic Heritage Museum, Seattle (1994). Photo by Lori Talcott.

the yield of the soil. These magical powers issuing from the *sølvmora* (silver mother) were believed to protect the worker in the silver mine but at the same time jealously guard the treasures hidden in the ground.[93] Another function of the *sølje* was to serve as a marker of age and status within the social group. Unmarried girls, for example, would mostly wear the so-called *slangesølje* ("snake" brooch featuring six arches mounted between two rings over an open background), while married women wore *bolesølje* (camber brooch made from

Lori Talcott. Traditional silver-gilt brooches: *bolesølje* (2011), *vestlandsølje* (2019), *filigransølje* with leaves (2017).
Photo by Lori Talcott.

elevated rings mounted on a plate).[94] Camber brooches have been documented in Norway and on the Continent since the Middle Ages, but usually in cast metal; silver filigree brooches appeared during the 1700s, presumably due to the discovery of silver in Norway.[95]

Among Norwegian Americans most of the social and symbolic meanings attached to the traditional make and use of *sølje* have largely been lost due to commercial mass production and fundamental changes in world view and cultural values. Even when purchasing expensive hand-made *sølje* from traditional silversmiths in Norway, ethnically motivated buyers usually foreground the decorative values rather than the historical contexts of ancient belief, symbolism and social custom inherent in this unique jewelry. None of this is surprising, of course: when an ethnic artifact crosses into another culture, it acquires new and different meanings in response to differences in cultural assumptions. To put it bluntly, a *sølje* worn on a reconstructed *bunad* in Seattle today wouldn't mean what it meant to someone getting married in a tightly-knit tradition community in rural Norway a century or two ago. Needless to say, the same cultural changes have occurred in Norway, too, and few Norwegians today associate *sølje* with its traditional meanings: the cultural border runs through Norway itself. Even an established silversmith like Hilde Nødtvedt struggles to motivate buyers to "invest" in her hand-made traditional creations as products of greater lasting value than most mass-produced consumer goods, realizing that if she paid herself at the same rate as a plumber, her work would find no buyers.

In Seattle, however, two extraordinary artists, Lori Talcott and Felicia Bauer, although not of Norwegian descent, have so thoroughly absorbed the

Bodice of Telemark *beltestakk* (belted skirt) decorated with a *slangesølje* (above) and a *bolesølje* (camber brooch) below. *Bunad* made by Linda Caspersen. Photo by author.

Setesdal folk costume from the 1860s decorated with silver buttons, chains and belt buckle and clasp. Owned by Linda Caspersen. Photo by author.

Left: silver, brass, and stainless steel, Smithsonian American Art Museum, Gift of Ina and Jack Kay, 2003. Center: photo-etched texts from *Beowulf, Caedmon's Hymn, Poetic* and *Prose Edda.* Right: the artist wearing the necklace.

traditions of making and using *sølje* that they might well be thought of as silversmiths in the pre-industrial Norwegian tradition. To be sure, their distinctly modern and "idiosyncratic work is not about producing historical replicas; rather it is about creating something new while working within the boundaries of the complex, visual language of Norwegian *sølje*-making in the past,"[96] albeit in individually different ways.

Lori Talcott took degrees in art and cultural history, jewelry and metal smithing before she apprenticed to Hilde Nødtvedt in 1990-1991, followed by five years of summer course work and research at *Raulandsakademiet* (Rauland Academy), a folk school in Vinje, Telemark, that offers courses in traditional and newer craft techniques. Starting in the 1990s, she established herself as a studio artist in her native Seattle, and in 2015 completed a graduate degree in visual arts. Her work in *sølje* was in the style and technique she had learned from her Norwegian teacher, working in filigree by hand-melting balls of silver, twining and braiding thread as small as 0.3mm in diameter, soldering hundreds of parts together in keeping with traditional designs, but improvising on the micro-level.

This traditional practice taught her "a complex, visual language, where one must become fluent in order to produce new iterations. Working within the boundaries of this language, one must not only understand the grammar and syntax in order to communicate, but also acquire a sufficient vocabulary in order to fully express oneself in an idiosyncratic way."[97] However, her research and immersion in a living tradition of folk jewelry in Norway taught her something even more significant for her development as an artist — an esthetic knowledge still passed from traditional master to apprentice, a knowledge that surprisingly engages "with contemporary theories on magic, the agency of objects, and the nexus of language and matter."[98] Talcott connected what she learned about traditional healing methods underlying the putative curative effects of *sølje* with James G. Frazer's concept of "sympathetic magic which may be called homeopathic or imitative," and is based on the principle that "like affects like."[99] Modern homeopathic medicine, formulated in 1796 by Samuel Hahnemann, proceeds on the assumption that a substance that causes symptoms of a disease in healthy people would cure similar symptoms in the sick. Furthermore, the homeopathic substances administered to patients are diluted to a point where they are no longer chemically traceable and what remains is a curative force that cannot be detected by physics, chemistry, or biology. Homeopathy and ethno-medicine practiced in the Nordic countries today owe their efficacy to the traditional understanding that the mental and emotional life of human individuals — their personalities, thoughts, feelings, and desires, are continuous beyond their own bodies with the surrounding natural environment thought to be endowed with life force or spirit. Magic consists of the practices of healers and wise folk to manipulate this force to benefit the community, or of witches to inflict harm.[100]

On this background, we can credit Talcott's statement that "formally and esthetically, (her) traditional work is the polar opposite of (her) contemporary work, but conceptually they operate in much the same way. Both rely on a participatory mode of making and activation, and both work from the premise that, in its deepest sense, ornament is about a completion and extension of self, with a magical and metaphysical dimension, as well as instrumental."[101] Talcott dissects the word homeopathy, breaking it down to its Greek roots, *homeo* meaning "same" or "like," and *pathos* meaning "suffering, feeling, emotion." The term "homeopathic" in her view thus evokes an associative mode of thinking conveyed through metaphor expressing the law of similars in sympathetic magic and healing. However, while "historically and cross-culturally systems of magic have customarily been practiced for the purpose of affecting the future, controlling the forces of nature, and protecting the wearer from physical or metaphysical harm," her work "is less about commanding external, metaphysical entities and more about a material metaphor having the capacity to affect the embodied experience of the wearer."[102]

For example, in the "homeopathic object" entitled *Brisings' Stole* (2002), the artist evokes the creative and destructive powers associated in Norse and Anglo-Saxon mythology with the goddess Freyja.[103] On the "leaves" of the necklace, Talcott photo-etched the medieval texts in which the necklace is described, thereby metaphorically invoking their presence in the object. The probable intent of the piece is to empower the wearer with the energies embodied in the stories about the goddess, a ritual gesture that would contradict the post-modernist denial of metaphysical reality. Talcott conceived of this piece in response to the wholesale destruction of sacred objects in war-torn Irak. In the

Lori Talcott 2015. "Synecdoche." Photo by Hank Drew.

age of the #MeToo movement and the struggle for gender equality, the symbolic meaning of that ritual gesture takes on renewed significance.

Another example of such homeopathic objects ("Synecdoche"), made from oxidized silver, mirror, and gelatin silver, was displayed in 2015 in a one-person exhibition at Sienna Patti Gallery in Lennox, Massachusetts. The image shows a polished, leaf-like silver object. At its center an eye looks back at the beholder cradling the object in her hand as if in meditation, reminding me of the life-changing instruction I received many decades ago from a Vedantic Swami, to meditate on the "eye of the Universal Christ."

Lori Talcott continues to create wearable, magical objects — in the traditional sense of magical — today. Her most recent work, a brooch entitled "Eye of the Beloved," for example, witnesses to the killing of George Floyd, as "the eternal, continuous gaze"[104] of the man looking at us from the clasp.

Bauer's connection to Scandinavia derives from the help Jewish people received from the Danes during World War Two and her early admiration of the progressive humanism of the Nordic countries. Exposure to Nordic art in museums and galleries in New York City, where she grew up, deepened when taking degrees in architecture at the Universities of Pennsylvania and Columbia. Following completion, she went to Scandinavia to see firsthand the work of the masters she so admired. During one of many visits, she met a Norwegian goldsmith who helped to deepen her understanding of the thousand-year-old *sølje* tradition. Bauer came to see that "while still remaining culturally significant to the majority of Norwegians (and to some active silversmiths and living tradition communities), the bulk of commercially visible forms of the tradition had now become codified through mechanical production and marketing in ways that fixed it more readily in the forms of its traditional past." Wondering how a "metals tradition as rich and significant as Norwegian *sølje* should continue its long process of evolution,"[105] led Bauer to embark on "Blue Ice Design," in an effort to find a current expression of the tradition for contemporary use.

Much of this work developed in the orbit of Norwegian architect Christian Norberg-Schulz, whose seminal book *Genius Loci: Towards a Phenomenology of Architecture* (1979)[106] made him a leading international figure in the development of phenomenological architectural theory, with an emphasis on the significance of place and its psychological implications for human life. Norberg-Schulz developed a theory of understanding architecture in concrete, existential terms, following Martin Heidegger's concept of "dwelling" as something more than shelter. The "spirit of a place" or dwelling gives symbolic meanings to "life situations" as something where "life takes place" and becomes a living process of constant reinterpretation of basic qualities inherent in a culture and its physical manifestations, as that life evolves. During the fourteen years she spent in Norway, Bauer eventually came to work as an architect for Snøhetta A.S. and, eventually, began the 'Blue Ice' workshop in Voss, together with the Norwegian friend with whom she originally began her exploration of the *solje* tradition. Snøhetta A.S. (named after a snow-covered mountain top in Gudbrandsdalen) is an international architecture, landscape, interior and brand design office based in Oslo and New York City with studios in San Francisco, Innsbruck, Paris, Hong Kong, Adelaide (Australia), and Stockholm. The firm describes itself as a collaborative architectural and landscape workshop dedicated to "enhanc(ing) our sense of surroundings, identity and relationship to others and the physical spaces we inhabit, whether feral or human-made."[107]

Norberg-Schulz was an influence at Snøhetta, making his presence felt on architectural projects being juried in competitions entered into by the firm. As Bauer puts it, according to Norberg-Schulz, what is typically Norwegian form, and the genius loci of the place that is Norway, "draws on the unique nature of the climate-driven Nordic light and its effect on a discontinuous web of spatial openings and closings within Norwegian forests, mountains and valleys. Norberg-Schulz refers to northern spaces as openings in this web of shadows and different from the bright object-exposing light of the European South." It is in this interplay of light and shadow that the continuity of matter and spirit finds its expression in traditional folk beliefs. Bauer puts it abstractly: "The North is a place of nuance, fluidity and mood, embodying tension in dynamic interplay," and she finds that "the contemporary forms of choice have more often been topological than figural…in keeping with the overwhelming presence of nature."[108] While in Norway, Bauer experimented with the varied repetition of related forms, operating as links in a process of natural growth and in keeping with the unique typology; specifically, "how light interacts with that form" to express "the dynamic fluidity of that light." To express this, she made use of the vocabulary of Scandinavian Modern Design that had begun to emerge at the beginning of and continued well into the twentieth century (1880-1980), alongside the modernist movement in Europe and America. It is "characterized by clear disciplined designs, inspired by nature, utilizes traditional materials/finishes and sculptural form while maintaining a high regard for the excellence of craftsmanship." As Bauer puts it, "Scandinavian Modernism is generally described as a design whose heart can be best found in winter," a time when the light becomes precious in Norway.

The two sets of brooches and ear studs below illustrate the artist's intent. The first ("Sun") was made in 2000 and the second ("Frost") followed in 2004.

"Sun," is modeled on the Norwegian *platering* (plate ring) fibula, using a traditional prong mechanism for attachment to clothing. The design makes use of repetitive shapes "which combine, stand alone or become absent spatial elements." The second and later set, called "Frost," more clearly represents the fluidity and dynamic interplay of light on its crystalline forms. When the brooch is worn, the light moves constantly around the highly polished, angled forms, changing emphasis with movement and the varied reflection of that light.

At present, Bauer continues her work in her studio in Seattle.

Boat Building

In 1992 my student Gry Løklingholm published the results of field study we did on three Norwegian American boat builders in the Pacific Northwest: Art Losvar, Paul Schweiss and Jay Smith,[109] all three of them "having built or continuing to build wooden boats in the tradition of Scandinavian shipwrights." The renowned Mukilteo Boat developed by the Losvar family "represented conservatism in the *informal transmission* of form and function, and *dynamism* in the evolution of the boat's (design)," meaning that they unselfconsciously brought their traditional skills from Norway to bear on the development of a new boat type in America. By contrast, "boats built by Paul Schweiss and Jay Smith manifest conservatism in their form and function, and dynamism in the way that tradition was transmitted," meaning that both Paul's and Jay's boats represent a self-conscious revival and transplantation of tradition from Scandinavia to the United States."[110] The distinction between "immigrant" and "ethnic" folklore made by George Schoemaker allows us to see the same difference between these three boat builders in yet another way.[111] When Art Losvar's grandfather, Paul Losvar, emigrated from the Alta region in northern Norway in 1879, he passed on in America the knowledge and skill of boat building he had acquired in the old country. Paul Schweiss and Jay Smith, on the other hand, both of part Norwegian descent but without direct access to immigrant boat building tradition, each made the conscious decision to go variously to Norway, Denmark and the Faroe Islands and there apprentice themselves to traditional shipwrights, and then carry their acquired skills back to the U.S. This parallels the experience of Norwegian American folk dancers, Hardanger fiddle players and makers, and many craftspeople, who went to Norway to immerse themselves in the traditions-based culture as it is practiced there today and brought their experience back to their communities in the Pacific Northwest.

The Losvars developed the Mukilteo Boat dynamically by combining traditional methods of lapstrake and carvel construction to create something new. Lapstrake construction was developed by Viking shipbuilders who worked without any plans or drawings, building hulls by relying solely on their hands and eyes like a sculptor who carries the necessary shape in his memory; they clinked the planks together with copper rivets, and subsequently inserted ribs after the hull had been fashioned. By contrast, carvel construction, first documented in Europe in the fifteenth century, involved pressing planks together edge to edge and calking the seams. These boats were built upside down on a frame skeleton of predetermined, measured and drawn design. Between 1905 and 1913, Paul Losvar built multiple 12-14 foot Viking-style lapstrake boats which he adapted from the narrow, shallow water river boats of Alta to the requirements of deep-water, offshore fishing; these he rented out to sports- and fishermen around Puget Sound. With the arrival of outboard motors in the 1920s, necessitating a transom from which to hang the engine, he changed his boat design to carvel construction with a high Norwegian style bow, producing 16-18 foot Mukilteo Boats at his Boat House. After Paul's death in the 1930s, the Boat House was taken over by his son George who passed it on to his own son, Art. Art continued building the Mukilteo Boat until the arrival of lower priced aluminum and fiberglass boats drove the traditional wooden boats from the market in the 1950s. Remarkably, the Losvars continued the Viking tradition of building the Mukilteo Boats by eye, without predetermined plans in the form of technical line-drawings or loftings, which are full-scale templates of all the pieces made prior to building a boat. In the 1940s, when they experimented with lofting designs, they found that the boat got wider than they wanted it, and they changed back to building without the aid of technical designs, relying only on their hands and eyes. The last Mukilteo Boat was built in 1948, and it continued in family use until Art's death in 2019.

Paul Schweiss and Jay Smith came to Scandinavian-style boat building indirectly, motivated by an interest in exploring their Norwegian ethnic heritage.

An article in *National Geographic* about traditional Norwegian boat builders spurred Paul to locate a master in Norway who would teach him, and he found two — one near Molde where he spent six months in 1974, the other in the Volda region, where he spent another six months in 1975. After returning to Tacoma he built more than 30 different small Norwegian and Danish style wooden pleasure boats, using his hands and eyes rather than line drawings or loftings, as he had learned from his Norwegian teachers. By 1981, however, Paul found that he could no longer compete with mass-produced aluminum or

fiberglass boats, and he had to sell his business. After interviewing him several times with Gry Løklingholm between 1990 and 1992, I lost contact with him, but discovered in 2020 that, since his retirement, Paul has built a new workshop and is looking forward to building boats again and teaching the craft. Why? Because, as both Paul Schweiss and Jay Smith came to realize over the years of building wooden boats in the Scandinavian tradition, these craft "represent a perfect fusion of form and function cultivated over the centuries."[112]

Jay Smith's first contact with Norwegian boat building occurred while he studied Norwegian at the University of Oslo in 1973 and visited relatives in Nordmøre. They showed him half-models and hand tools used for all boat construction before the industry switched to steel in 1965. The unforgettable functional beauty of those boat models brought Jay back to Norway in 1977-1978, where his relatives helped him find a traditional boat builder in Aspøya in Freifjord. After apprenticing there for eighteen months, Jay returned to the U.S. in 1979, where he built small lapstrake boats in Wisconsin for three years. He was commissioned to build a ship's boat for the *Hjemkomst*, a replica Viking ship that sailed to Norway in 1982; then he continued his training in the Faroe Islands for seven months, followed by a five-month stint in Denmark. Back in the U.S. in 1983, Jay worked as director of a county-funded project in Pennsylvania involving developmentally disabled youth in building plywood

river boats. By 1987 Jay and his family settled in Anacortes, Washington, where he first worked in a boat shop, but soon set up his own shop called Aspøya Boats, where he could construct wooden boats more than thirty feet in length in the Scandinavian tradition. This is where Gry Løklingholm and I interviewed him in 1990-1992. When I returned to his shop in 2020, it became apparent that Jay Smith had continued plying his craft in constructing Danish, Faroese and Norwegian boats, in each case using the techniques and tools he had brought with him from Scandinavia.

Over the years, Jay has organized a Friday Guild of volunteers who come to his shop to build a variety of Norwegian-style boats. These have included a

Naturally grown mast step from single tree

ten-foot pram of Western Norwegian design and a 19.5 foot Nordmøre style *geitbåt* (goat boat) built from wide planks fastened with rivets and treenails (wooden dowels), the fastening system that has been used in Norway for some twelve hundred years. A local blacksmith handcrafted the gudgeon (female part) and pintel (male part) for the interpivoting connection of the boat rudder, and the boat was rigged in the style developed in the 1500s. A third boat built by the guild was an 18-foot Nordfjord *færing* (from Old Norse *feræringr*, meaning "four-oaring"), a regional type of clinker-built boat, with wide overlapping strakes fastened together with rivets and treenails to form a hull that was filled with frames grown naturally in selected trees for maximum strength and minimal mass. The planks for the boat were carved with adzes from flitches split from logs rather than sawn, because the historical model for this boat developed before there were any sawmills.

While this burdened the builder with additional labor, it also allowed selective use of the grain pattern and twists in the wood to lend strength and durability to the planks. The strakes to be mounted at the aft and forward ends, were bent by steam from boiling water. It would take about fifty minutes to soften the wood and then the builder had approximately six minutes to install the plank on the boat before it cooled and relaxed into the intended shape, typically overnight. Construction of the Nordfjord *færing* goes back to the small boats interred together with the Gokstad ship found in a burial mound near Oslo in 1880 and dated to around 890 A.D. It resembles the type of boats still used in much of Western and Northern Norway as small fishing vessels and occasionally for racing. For centuries, the *færing* served coastal communities in Norway pretty much the way a Model-T Ford served rural communities in America in the early 20th century: people would use them to go to town, church, weddings and funerals, or to haul hay across the fjord. In addition to oars, *færings* could also carry a small sail (traditionally a square sail). Eventually the rudder was repositioned from the starboard side to the sternpost.

In 2018, Jay completed the 36-foot Viking ship replica Polaris (for comparison, the Gokstad ship was 78.1 feet long) on commission for an Irishman residing in the Boston area. The Polaris, now in Gloucester, Massachusetts, is used as a charter day sailer for small groups and families. Longer charters follow the sandy coastline of Ipswich Bay for a maximum of ten guests, plus a crew of two. For comparison, the Gokstad ship had room for 32 oarsmen, while the Polaris uses oars and sail.

Currently, Jay is working on his largest Viking ship yet, the 56-foot Valkyrie, its design based on models of ships from the late 10-11th centuries. By this time, Viking ships had achieved a highly refined form, with hulls more shapely and elegant than before, less extreme in transition from their water line to the freeboard, and the lapstrakes fused with treenails rather than lashed as in the earlier Oseberg and Gokstad ships. The Valkyrie was commissioned by two Danish Americans, David and Erik Knudsen, father and son (the skipper), who usually live in Delaware and Pennsylvania, but come to the West Coast seasonally. They intend to use the ship as a charter vessel on Puget Sound, the South Sound and Shilshole Bay for summer tourists, and maybe Lake Union in the winter. Their goal is to work with disadvantaged youth on extended voyages, to teach them how to work as a team, build self-confidence and establish personal goals. This ship will have a crew of two, plus the skipper, and will be equipped with a traditional square sail.

Like Paul Schweiss, Jay Smith builds Norwegian-style boats because it gives him a sense of ethnic identity. Like Paul, he works intuitively without line drawings and loftings, and constructs drawings after the fact for approval by the Coast Guard for use of the boats in public waters. He thinks of himself as a sculptor, "trusting the eye, building a symmetry, and creating a form" within certain traditional, flexible and organic

frameworks regarding size and shape, rather than as a commercial ship builder working from design specifications. He insists that he would be building boats even if he could not make a living doing it. The economic arrangements supporting his work are always tenuous and unpredictable. For instance, one of the members of his Friday Guild bought the materials for building the Nordfjord *færing*, and she will take possession of the boat for her own use after she has helped build it. Over the years a number of boats have been commissioned by "eccentrics" who understand the beauty and deep cultural history of these exquisite craft. Jay also teaches boat building at various schools, for example, at the Center for Wooden Boats in Seattle, the Northwest School of Wooden Boatbuilding in Port Townsend, or the Wooden Boat School in Brooklin, Maine, but finds the task challenging and exhausting. How do you teach young people whose lives are dominated by virtual realities and push buttons? How do you get them to understand that it may take two hours to hone a tool before you can put it to use? How to work with natural materials and design traditions that are hundreds of years old and reveal a profound understanding of how water and vessels interact? And, yet, he says: "This is meant to be. I was accepted by master boat builders in Norway; they taught me, and now it is my turn to pass it on — an intrinsic obligation I have accepted joyfully." In 2020, Jay Smith received a grant from the Heritage Arts Apprenticeship Program (Center for Washington Cultural Traditions) to teach his craft to the next generation of boat builders.

Food Ways

An important identifier of Norwegian ethnicity is food. To quote Swedish chef and food writer, Magnus Nilsson: "Food is an undeniable and unavoidable marker of culture and society."[113] So, what ethnic foods do Norwegian Americans buy today, which of these do they prepare at home, and from where do they get their skills to prepare such foods? Nowhere is the distinction between ethnic and immigrant folklore more pronounced than in traditions about food ways. The immigrants who arrived in America before the 1930s came mostly from farms and homesteads where the daily fare was produced at home in quantities just large enough to provide an adequate diet until the next harvest.[114] Rural households in pre-industrial Norway, whether inland or along the coasts and fjords, were self-sufficient in the sense that almost all the foods they relied on for survival came from the labor of their own hands in fishing and hunting, growing and wildcrafting, and in preparing and preserving what they ate. Today, the opposite is the case: almost all the foods consumed in Norwegian American households, or in Norway for that matter, come from producers outside the home, either in ready-to-eat form or as ingredients from which to make traditional dishes. The love of certain ethnic and regional foods, and the skills required to prepare them, are often handed down in families by word of mouth and by example, or learned from Norwegian cookbooks or in heritage courses offered by ethnic organizations.[115] But unlike the immigrants who came to America during the nineteenth and early twentieth centuries, very few Norwegian Americans today still produce the raw materials of their own food, nor are their food choices dictated by the opportunities and limitations of regional food traditions, producer skill, seasonal work rhythms, soil fertility or climate. Most of the foods ethnic Norwegians want are available commercially in specialty stores in America, such as Scandinavian Specialties in Ballard,[116] which has been in business since 1962, owned and managed by successive generations of Norwegian immigrants.

The wares sold by this and similar stores in the Pacific Northwest cover the whole range of "Norwegian foods" mentioned by informants for this study, and they can be divided into five major groups, listed here in the order of their importance to the traditional Norwegian diet: fresh and processed fish; porridges and soups; bread and other bakery goods from unleavened breads such as *lefse* (thin pancakes made from rolled flour and potato dough), *knekkebrød* (rye crisp), *flatbrød* (flat bread), fermented breads, and cakes; fresh and fermented cheeses; fresh and cured meats; condiments, jellies, jams, juices, sweets and chocolates. Some of these foods are produced locally in the Seattle area and elsewhere. Fresh baked goods, for example, are made by Scandia Bakery and Lefse Factory in Stanwood. Scandinavian Specialties prepares many kinds of Norwegian-style fresh sausages such as *medisterpølse* (pork sausage), *rullepølse* (rolled and pressed sausage from pork belly and various herbs), and cured meats, as well as *spekesild* (pickled herring), in house. Many other products, however, are imported from Norway in the form of mass-produced, ready-to-eat foods. Fish products and flatbread, for example, are manufactured by Orkla, a Norwegian conglomerate operating mostly in the Nordic region,

Eastern Europe, Asia, and the U.S. Another mass producer of the foods sold in the Ballard store is the Norwegian food giant Toro, which last year sold some 140 million processed food units. Much of the iconic *geitost* (goat or "brown" cheese), which had its origin in the small mountain dairies of Gudbrandsdal, is now fabricated by TINE, Norway's largest distributor and exporter of dairy products. Most of the candies and milk chocolates, such as *Kvikk Lunsj (*Quick Lunch*)*, are made in Norway by Freia which was founded in 1889 in Oslo, and in 1993 was purchased by Kraft Foods, an American company. Popular condiments such as caviar paste, cod roe spread, salmon spread and mayonnaise are produced by Mills of Norway (another American company), and other fabricators.

In pre-industrial, rural Norway, food practices and traditions were intimately tied to daily and seasonal work rhythms. On a typical homestead, daily meal schedules reflected a long work day, starting with *åbit* (early bite) also called *fastanbetan* (fasting bite), consisting of a sip of brandy or milk and a piece of bread eaten before animal chores between 4-6 am, followed by *dugurden* (morning meal), most often porridge, between 7-8 am, followed in turn by *non* (afternoon meal) eaten around 2-3 pm and consisting of meat, herring or other fish. Later this meal was often referred to as *middag* (midday meal) and workers were allowed a two hours' rest. The daily food schedule normally ended with *eftasverd* (evening meal), often porridge, bread and dairy products.[117]

Seasonal and church calendars also had a profound effect on food traditions.[118] During Lent when Christians celebrated *feittirsdagen* (Fat Tuesday) or *askonsdagen* (Ash Wednesday), meat and fatty foods were not allowed, but in modern times *fastlavnsboller* (sweet baked rolls) took their place. Special Christmas and Easter fare included *kjøttmølje* (crumbled flatbread and meat fried in fat), served during the day on Christmas Eve, for example, while the main festive evening meal featured *risengryngrøt* (rice porridge), *lutefisk* (cod treated in lye and boiled), *torsk* (fresh cod), or *ribbe* (spare ribs). In Sogn and Fjordane, boiled pig's head and potato dumplings were common on Fat Tuesday. In Hedmark, it was traditional on Good Friday to eat cooked herring and herring soup; on Easter Day, veal, milk soup, as well as *kjeleost* (pot cheese), egg dishes

— the hens started laying in spring — and pancakes. On the coast, the traditional Easter food was mostly fish — most often *lutefisk*. Beer was a rarity at Easter, but other celebrations such as weddings, baptisms, birthdays, and funerals required the hosts to provide plentiful supplies of home-brewed beer and *akevitt* (brandy), while the main dishes were provided by the guests in a potluck. April 14, which traditionally marked the beginning of the summer season, and June 21, which marked midsummer, called *jonsokdagen* (St. John's Day), a favorite day for weddings, were celebrated by serving *rømmegrøt* (cream porridge). After completion of the hay, potato, or grain harvest, farmers also rewarded their workers with a festive meal of *rømmegrøt*.

After the holidays, when rural life returned to the rhythm of *strieskjorta og havrelefse* (sackcloth shirt and oat cakes), the daily work schedule also required adjustments of meals, because the men would often be absent from home for weeks or months to go fishing or hunting, work in the forests, or for several days to work in the fields clearing land, planting or harvesting. The women would provision the men with salt pork and dried meat, flatbread, porridge, butter and *pultost* (soft, sharp spreadable cheese made from sour skimmed milk), beer left over from the holidays, sour milk and buttermilk. At the *seter* (summer mountain dairy), the dairymaids used waffle irons to make waffles to supplement fresh dairy products, such as *dravle* (cooked curds and whey, a by-product of making *geitost*). If the farm had sent its cow to the *seter* for the summer, and there was no fresh milk at home, the household relied on *surprim* (semi-cooked, i.e. pasteurized, milk that would stay palatable for an indefinite time). Before spring planting, bread had to be baked in quantities large enough to last the summer, a project that often involved several farms working together. Women would bake *flatbrød, lefse, skrivarbrød* (writing bread), a thin round cake baked on an iron plate and then given an extra coating of very thin batter on which to draw a line pattern), and *hardingkake* (Hardanger cake), and the breads were stored in great stacks in the *stabbur* (a storage building built on stilts to keep rats out). In the fall, after the grain was harvested, threshed and ground, another round of baking *flatbrød* and *lefse* provided bread for the coming winter.

Fish, of course, has always been a major part of the traditional Norwegian diet:[119] herring along the entire Atlantic coast, mackerel in the South, cod and rose fish, also called haddock or perch, in the North, fresh water trout, perch and salmon inland. The cultural habit of eating fresh fish is continued today, both in Norway and among Norwegian Americans in the Pacific Northwest, and here they have ample access to fish from Puget Sound and Alaskan stocks. In rural Norway, however, fish was so common that in the past agricultural workers would complain about the dominance of fish in their diet.[120] In the 1960s, I heard fellow students at the University of Oslo grumble that "fish is fish, but meat is food."

Among Norwegian Americans, *lutefisk* is still considered the quintessential ethnic food and is consumed widely in Lutheran churches and fraternal lodges. Traditionally, *lutefisk* was made from air-dried and salted cod, ling or burbot, which allowed for longterm storage without refrigeration or freezing. To rehydrate the dried stockfish for eating, it was pickled in lye and then watered over several days to remove the lye, giving the fish a gelatinous texture. The lye was made by cooking sifted ashes mixed in water. The lye was ready "when it burned on the tongue… and really good if the housewife got mad… When making lye it was a good idea to really tease her."[121] As a part of the Christmas tradition, *lutefisk* was mostly eaten with boiled potatoes, cooked dried peas and white sauce. In modern stores, *lutefisk* is usually offered frozen, rehydrated and ready to eat. Another modern favorite among Norwegian Americans is sardines, actually a small species of herring (Lat. sprattus sprattus) caught in coastal and fjord waters, filleted, smoked and packed in tins in olive oil, to be enjoyed especially on *knekkebrød* (rye crisp) and *flatbrød* (flat bread). Norwegian Americans also like to buy fish cakes and fish balls. A recipe for "old-fashioned fish balls" (1860) from Møre and Romsdal calls for pounding coalfish or haddock together with some flour, salt and caraway, and thinning the dough with milk or fish broth. Balls were formed by hand and boiled, and served with fried pork and sour milk.[122] A fancy modern recipe for homemade fish balls, by contrast, provides for white fish and stock, eggs, cream, flour, butter, curry powder, and pastry shells in which to serve the fish balls, garnished with asparagus tips, small shrimp and slices of lemon. Most Norwegian Americans, however, prefer to buy canned fishballs and eat them with potatoes and green peas, for instance. Another favorite Norwegian American food is *gravlaks* (buried salmon), so-called because traditionally, salted salmon fillets were layered with dill and buried for several days wrapped in burlap, until fully autolyzed. Today most Norwegian Americans buy ready-made *gravlaks* that has been cured in a modern refrigerator.

Porridges, soups and stews were another mainstay of traditional diets. Oat and barley porridge utilized the grains grown in Norway for many centuries. Until 1,000 A.D., four grain types dominated in the Nordic countries: barley and rye were the oldest, wheat and oats more recent. During the Iron Age (500 A.D. – 1050 A.D.), rye became the most commonly used grain for bread until the beginning of the 20th century, when wheat became more prevalent. *Rømmegrøt* (cream porridge) made from heavy sour cream, was a delicacy prepared for special occasions and holidays, and is today considered an iconic Norwegian dish. The many recipes for *rømmegrøt* differ, depending on the region of the country. Traditional soups ranged from fish, pea and potato soups to all kinds of milk-based soups. Today, most of the porridges and soups can be bought as pre-fabricated mixes.

Bread and other baked goods: "And Give Us Today Our Daily Bread." In Norway, as in other cultures the world over, bread has played a major role not only in the diet of most people, but has also been regarded as a sacred "staff of life."[123] Since the early history of Norway, two types of bread have been documented: the white wheat loaves consumed in the homes of noblemen and wealthy city dwellers, and the heavy, coarse breads eaten by common folk in the rural districts. Barley, the oldest grain, dominated in the mountainous northern parts of the country, while oats were were cultivated in southern Norway. Wheat was mostly imported from warmer climates further south and was used for festive occasions by the rich, and in the bread used for Holy Communion.

Early on, barley and oat breads were made from crushed grain kneaded into a flat, unleavened cake baked on a flat stone by the fire or in the ashes. These flat cakes, called *askestompe* (ash stump; also called *glohane* (ember cock), *glohoppe* (ember mare), *glokake* (ember cake), or *hellekake* (stone cake),[124] were used as edible plates for fish, meats and vegetables. The need to preserve them for extended periods led to the development of *flatbrød* (flatbreads). By the 1500s, when millstones powered by waterwheels were developed, and grain could be ground more quickly and in larger quantities, leaven made from fermented hops came into use, to make longer-lasting sourdough rye bread. The bread was baked in ovens built from fire-proof field stones installed either at the back of the house and connected to the in-house fireplace, or built in a separate *bryggehus* (brewing house) which, as the name implies, doubled as the place to brew beer. It would take about three hours to warm the baking oven by burning wood inside the baking chamber. The oven was ready for baking when the stones had turned white all over. Then the ashes were swept out with a broom and the baking floor washed with a wet cloth attached to the stick. Since the grain mills depended on the good flow of water typically occurring in fall and spring, most of the bread was baked during those two seasons for bulk storage.

In the mid-18th century potatoes were introduced into Norway, thereby not only eliminating chronic vitamin deficiencies throughout the country, but also leading to the invention of *lefse,* in various regions called *tunnbrød, kling, klining or krotekake,* all meaning very thin, crispy breads that could be stored for years. Initially *lefse* was made entirely from potatoes, but now this iconic ethnic food is also made from flour, milk and eggs, buttered, sugared and folded. There are about as many traditional recipes of *lefse* as there are cultural regions in Norway. Generally speaking, potato *lefse* continue to be prevalent in Eastern Norway, flour *lefse* (also referred to as *Hardanger lefse*) in Western Norway. Today this ethnic food is eaten as a party sweet, but also as *lefserull* (wrap) stuffed with savory fillings much like a tortilla. *Lefse* are baked on special flat and round iron pans called *takke* (griddle).

Another variant of long-lasting dry breads developed over time was called *kavring* (rusk) or *tvebak* (twice-baked). These could be stored indefinitely and therefore particularly suitable as provision for ships' crews going on long voyages. Another form of long-lasting, storable bread, called *knekkebrød* (crisp bread), was introduced to Norway from central Sweden, where it had been a major part of

Home baking *lefse* today. (From: Magnus Nilsson, 489-490.

the diet since about 500 A.D. It was made in large rounds with a hole at the center so that the bread could be stored on poles suspended horizontally under the ceiling to keep it safe from rats. Like other storable breads, *knekkebrød* was baked just twice a year. Traditionally it was made from rye, salt, and water; today, however, it often contains wheat and other whole grains and spices, and is sprinkled with sesame seeds. The characteristic bubbles on the surface of *knekkebrød*, which traditionally were created by mixing snow or cracked ice into the dough, which then evaporated during the baking, today are introduced mechanically by pushing the dough through an extruder.

Norwegian Americans also love the many traditional bakery goods that satisfy the sweet tooth, including *lefse* sprinkled with sugar and cinnamon. Many of these delicacies continue to be made in Norwegian American homes, or are sold in specialty stores. The list of baked goods provided by respondents for this study are topped by the following: *vafler* (waffles), *krumkake* (thin, delicate wafers rolled into cones and filled with whipped cream), *fattigmann* (poor man), *bløtkake* (layer cake), *kransekake* (wreath cake), *julekake* (Christmas cake), and *Yule-log* (Christmas cake in the shape of a log).

Only the first three confections represent traditions going back to the rural culture of pre-industrial Norway. As mentioned before, *vafler* (waffles) were baked on a waffle iron over the open fire. In Ryfylke, the dough consisted variously of wheat, barley, or oat flour, even leftover porridge or potatoes, mixed with flour, milk and cream, sugar, salt, soda, perhaps spiced with cardamom and cinnamon, and fried on an iron greased with pork fat. Today, specialty stores offer ready-made waffle mix or even frozen waffles. According to a recipe from Buskerud, *krumkaker* were traditionally concocted from barley flour, butter and sugar and baked on a large round iron; sometimes they were rolled and filled, at other times eaten as flat cakes. A recipe from Oppland for *fattigmann* (known as crullers outside of Scandinavia) calls for 10 eggs, 10 spoons of sugar, 15 of thick cream, plus a little ginger, to make a dough that can be rolled with a pin, and then deep-fried in lard. Doesn't sound like a poor man's dessert to me! Today, *fattigmann* is flavored with cognac, lemon juice, Ättika vinegar (a solution of acetic acid in water also called white vinegar), cut into knot-shaped pieces and, after frying, covered with powdered sugar, plain or cinnamon sugar and served with coffee as a snack, or with whipped cream and jam. Crullers are made unleavened or leavened with baking powder, baking soda or with baker's ammonia.[125]

Bløtkake (layer cake) is a modern creation offered in pastry shops, but some people still make them at home. Basically a sponge cake filled with vanilla custard, berries and whipped cream, it is considered de rigueur for birthday parties and at Midsummer. *Kransekake* (wreath cake), another festive creation served at weddings, birthday parties, Christmas and New Year's Eve, is a pastry made from sugar, egg whites, almond marzipan, and a pinch of salt, and placed on a baking sheet in circular logs, with each circle being a slightly smaller diameter than the previous one. The baked rings are stacked on top of each other into a rounded pyramid and covered with icing.[126] *Julekake* (Christmas cake) is a yeast wheat bread filled with dried and candied fruit traditionally served during the Christmas holidays.[127] The last confection to be mentioned here, the so-called *Yule-log*, probably owes its inclusion among Norwegian ethnic foods to faulty etymology. The sweet dessert in the form of a chocolate covered roulade originated in France and the French-speaking parts of Belgium, Switzerland and Canada where it is called *Bûche de Noël* (log of Noel) since it looks like a small tree trunk. In England it came to be known as Yule-log because, as historian Henry Bourne (1694–1733) argued in *Antiquitates Vulgares* (1725), the *Yule-Log* harks back to a physical log being ritually burned at winter solstice by prehistoric Germanic tribes. So how did this ancient Germanic ritual that supposedly gave birth to a French confection end up as a Norwegian Christmas cake? Svale Solheim, my teacher in folklore studies at the University of Oslo, surmised that as descendants of Norwegian immigrants lost command of the Norwegian language, they also lost knowledge of some of the non-Christian aspects of Christmas. They confused "Yule-log" with the traditional concept of *julelaug* (Jul-bath), also known as *sjelebad* (soul-bath).[128] The Jul- or soul-bath was based on the folk belief that at solstice spirits of nature and the dead would haunt the living, and that it was wise to propitiate them by offering to share the ritual sauna and some of the Christmas fare with them.[129] This belief was reflected both in legend form (legend type ML 6015) and folktales (AT 1161).[130] The modern Yule-log is made from devil's food cake mix, and topped with whipped frosting.

Dairy & Cheese: Among the numerous cheeses displayed in the Seattle store, the most iconic is no doubt *geitost* (goat cheese), also called *brunost* (brown cheese), which today is "considered an important part of Norwegian gastronomical and cultural identity and heritage."[131] Historically, however, *geitost* is a fairly recent and local innovation, dating back to 1862 when a young enterprising dairy maid in Gudbrandsdal experimentally added some sweet cream to whey and boiled it until it was brown.[132] Twenty years later, she and her husband had the idea to mass-produce the cheese and market it in Oslo, which they did with great success. In 1933, Anne Håve received the Norwegian Medal of Honor as the originator of *Gudbrandsdalosten* (Gudbrandsdal Cheese), as it was then called. This sweet cheese is made by caramelizing whey through boiling. The effect came to be called the Maillard reaction by the French chemist, who in 1912 described non-enzymatic browning as a complex series of reactions between amino acids and reducing sugars at increased temperatures. Brown cheese doesn't require maturation, and can be kept fresh in a cool place for several weeks.

Jahn Ekenaes (1847-1920), "Churning Butter," 1908

Ekte Geitost (Genuine Goat Cheese) is the leading cheese sold by Norwegian American specialty stores in the U.S., but of course it is now mass-produced by the two giant dairies, TINE and Synnøve, as are all the other Norwegian cheeses offered, for example, by Scandinavian Specialties in Seattle. Among these the most popular are: *nøkkelost* (key cheese), a factory-made version of Dutch Leyden cheese flavored with cumin; *ridderost* (knight cheese), a much imitated Norwegian invention of a semi-soft, nutty cheese coated with a rust-colored annatto rind; *Jarlsberg* (Jarlsberg cheese), a Norwegian version of Swiss *Emmentaler* (Emmental cheese), originally introduced into Norway by Swiss cheesemakers in the 1830s, where it thrived for several years but then disappeared from the market, until re-invented at the Agricultural

University of Norway and licensed for mass-production by TINE, and by now apparently the most imported cheese in the world; *gulost* (yellow cheese), a Norwegian imitation of Dutch gouda; and *Snøfrisk* (snow-fresh), a spreadable, cream-like white goat cheese flavored variously with juniper berry, dill and other herbs, forest mushrooms and garlic, developed by TINE for the 1994 Winter Olympics in Lillehammer, Norway.

It is no surprise that the Norwegian cheeses offered in specialty stores in the U.S. are almost all long fermented and enzymatically stable cheeses that will survive shipment over long distances and extended storage on store shelves. These cheeses are of necessity factory-made in order to serve the mass market. An American subsidiary of TINE located in Ohio, for example, produced between 5 and 10 million pounds of Jarlsberg in 2004 alone.[133] The story of cheese making in historical tradition communities in rural Norway, however, is quite different.

In the naturally managed farm households in 19th-century Norway, dairy played a large role. Except for iron kettles, implements and tools were simple, mostly made of durable juniper wood. Cleaning made use of river sand and boiled juniper wash and took place stream-side. Fresh milk was allowed to ferment in shallow basins in a sheltered place before the cream was removed for butter-churning. Butter and cheese were mostly made during the short summer season when cows and goats were sent to the mountain farms (*seter*) to benefit from the rich forest pastures. *Kusleppdagen* (cow release day), was a festive and often chaotic day when the cattle that had been confined to the stable all winter, were moved first to nearby pastures and then to the mountains often miles away.

The task of preparing people, often the teenage members of the household, and outfitting everybody with food, tools, clothing and other needs for the summer, was exacting. Once arrived at the *seter,* it was customary to knock on the door and ask the nature spirits for permission to enter, and to nail a horseshoe or something else made of iron over the door as a protection against hostile powers. Besides churning cream into butter, cooking fresh and sour milk and whey into cheese, the herders would use portable spindles to make thread or yarn for knitting and weaving, or cook ashes into lye for making soap from animal fats. Butter was the most highly prized dairy product, both for food and trade. Unlike today, both the cream and milk were soured before processing into butter and cheese, for durability and flavor. The butter was churned in a tall, vertical *stavkjerne* (stave churn) standing on the floor, or in a horizontal *sveivekjerna* (crank churn) placed on a rack. After the butter separated from the buttermilk, it was washed by hand in cold water to express all the remaining liquid and kneaded until smooth and soft, then salted heavily for longterm storage in a cool cellar. It was common to sacrifice a little butter to the *usynlige* (invisible) to thank them and enlist their help. Folk beliefs surrounding the success or failure of dairying reflected the general sense of dependence on, and fear of, nature spirits,[134] as well as concern that envious neighbors might steal the butter right out of the churn.[135]

After making butter from the cream, the fresh skim milk was processed into *søtost* (white cheese), soured skim milk into *knaost* (cottage cheese). The fresh whey was caramelized into *mysost* (whey cheese), also called *brunost* (brown cheese). The sour whey was cooked into *prim* (whey cheese) or *surprim* (whey cheese reduced by further cooking). In a class by itself was *gammelost* (old sour milk cheese), a long-fermented, aged cheese that required the addition of *tette* (starter) to thicken the milk, and *kjese* (rennet) to initiate the curdling process. *Tette* was extracted from the leaves of *Tettegras* (Butterwort, Lat. pinguicula vulgaris), which were soaked in cooked or fresh milk until the milk solidified into a soft dough, of which a couple spoonfuls were added to the milk. *Kjese* was made from the lining of a calf's abomasum (third stomach), and the scrapings sewn back into the stomach pouch to dry. At cheese making time, the reusable *kjese* was soaked in whey, which was then added to the milk to precipitate curdling. *Gammelost*, aged for minimally two months in a cool cellar, was considered the pinnacle of Norwegian cheese making in pre-industrial Norway.

As described above, today fresh milk white cheese has been replaced by industrial brands of aged cheeses of different origins. Cottage cheese remains popular in mass-produced form. The caramelized brown cheeses, called *geitost* (goat cheese) or *brunost* (brown cheese) depending on the proportion of goat's or cow's milk in the cheese, are the most iconic Norwegian cheeses today. *Prim* is today the general name for a reduced sweetened whey product that is very popular in Scandinavia as a sandwich spread, especially among children, and is sold in aluminum containers that look like old-fashioned toothpaste tubes.[136] Besides fresh and aged cheeses, traditional dairy products in Norway included some foods that are still produced non-commercially today, among them *dravle* (simmered curds and whey), *tjukkmelk* (thick milk), and *kalvedans* (calf dance). In North Trøndelag, *ekte dravle* (real curds and whey) was a preferred *seter* food made from reduced whey to which *tette* had been added. In a modern version, *dravle* is made from fresh milk thickened with cream and eggs and boiled over medium heat until caramelization, and served with sugar and cinnamon.[137] Likewise, *tjukkmelk*, in some places today referred to as *soll* (cultured milk), which was traditionally served at the *seter* as a simple meal any time of the day, is still commonly served for lunch, with pieces of flatbread broken into the cultured milk.[138] *Kalvedans*, a baked colostrum pudding made from the first milk from a cow that had just given birth, was in traditional Norway a source of rich pancakes reminiscent of thick scrambled eggs.[139] The modern version is at times flavored with cinnamon or cardamon and topped with cream and jam. On our farm it is a celebratory dish whenever a new calf is born.

Meats: Besides the *rullepølse* and *medisterpølse* mentioned above, the display cases of the Ballard food store routinely contain other traditional-looking meats, such as *pinnekjøtt* (stick mutton), a Christmas Eve delicacy of mutton ribs that originated in Western Norway, where it was typically steamed for three hours in a kettle over a bed of birch sticks, and then roasted on a stick over an open fire or in a very hot cast iron pan; or *fenalår*, a salt-cured, dried leg of mutton once most common in Setesdal. The method of preserving the mutton reminds us that in the absence of freezers in pre-industrial Norway, drying, pickling, curing and smoking were the only methods to keep meat in extended storage. In cooking it was added to pea or barley soup, together with carrots and rutabaga, as Sunday food or for guests, or slices were carved from the leg to provision farmers, hunters or forest workers laboring away from home.

Like all other work processes on the farm, butchering was a seasonal event which determined what meats would be available throughout the year, and in what form.[140] At the end of the summer, when farmers would bring their cows, goats and sheep back down from the mountain dairies, they would have to decide how many animals to slaughter and how many to carry through the winter. Winter forage was difficult to collect and store and it was important to avoid *vårknipe* (spring pinch), that is, a shortage of hay, leaves and branches to feed by the end of winter. An average-sized farm would slaughter one cow, eight to ten sheep and a couple of pigs. To avoid food shortages, it was equally important that every part of a slaughter animal be utilized, "snout to tail"; there was no such thing as "offal." Innards, guts, stomachs, ligaments, skins, hoofs, tallow, fats, all found their use, providing not only high quality food, but also wool for clothing; fur for coats and blankets; leather for shoes, harness and rope; sinews and pig bristle for sewing leather coats, sails, and shoes; horn stuffers, gut casings and membranes for sausages; oil and grease for tools, guns and clocks; fuel for lamps and tallow for candles; fats for healing salves; horn for combs, spoons and other implements; cow tails for milk filters; thin lamb, goat and calf hides for sewing flour sacks. Slaughter tools were simple and few: wooden troughs, barrels and tubs carved from tree trunks and laid in water for tightness. In the absence of meat grinders, meat was chopped for sausage with axes and double-bladed knives. Brines were made from salt. Butchering usually took three days: the first to slaughter, stir and salt the blood for sausages, clean and scald intestines, stomachs, organs and edible chitterlings; the second day to break the sides into different cuts, carefully following the muscle groups, and salt and brine primary cuts; the third day to make sausage. Slaughter normally took place during the first cold days in November, at a waxing moon and high tide to make the meat more durable and "fuller."

There were four basic methods for preserving meats, often used in combination: drying, curing, pickling, and smoking. *Tørkjøtt* (dried meat) was brined overnight and then hung up to keep for several years. *Speket grisehode* (cured pig's head) was brined for 2-3 weeks and then dried and smoked. *Sylteflesk,* pickled pig's feet, snout, ears, and cheeks, was soaked in water for several days, then boiled and pickled in brine. *Persesylte* (pickled pork) was made from pig's head, trimmings, belly meat and sometimes small portions of veal, packed in a cloth inside a wooden bowl, layers of pork rinds followed by pork and veal, salt, herbs, slivered almonds (in southern Norway), topped with more pork rinds, tied together with string, cooked in broth, then pressed between planks weighted with stones, and finally stored in salt brine. *Rullepølse* (rolled sausage) were pieces of mutton or beef sides, salted and filled with herbs, rolled and sewn together, and brined. *Spekepølse* (smoked sausage) was made from pork, mutton or beef, chopped with pork fat, salted, herbed and spiced, and stuffed in large intestines, brined for three days and then smoked with juniper. *Mòrrpølse (*chopped sausage*)* was made mostly from innards and trimmings, stuffed in intestines, brined or rubbed with salt and hung to dry. *Grisesmør* (pork fat) was washed to remove all traces of blood, chopped and cooked for 2-3 hours, then filtered through a cloth and, after cooling, washed and kneaded in sweet milk, salted and used like butter on *flatbrød*, sourdough bread and potato pancakes.

Not surprisingly, most of these traditional meats and sausages are still available in specialty stores and some restaurants, especially in Scandinavia, but the ingredients have changed to the degree that modern eaters tend to recoil from innards (which nutritionally speaking actually are the most valuable parts of the animal),[141] justified partly because modern, industrial, chemical-centered methods of raising meat animals compromises the health and purity of the product. *Mòrrpølse*, for example, which traditionally was made from organ meats and blood, today is made commercially from all-muscle mutton, beef, pork and game, and typically spiced with multiple seasonings, garlic and chili pepper.[142] It is often served as a side dish accompanying *pinnekjøtt*. *Medisterpølse* now contains potato starch and milk for a smoother texture, and multiple spices including allspice, cloves, peppercorns, marjoram, sage, and mace.[143] *Persesylte* is still brined, cooked and pressed but mostly is made from pork shoulder rather than from the head, thus missing the opportunity to use the whole animal.[144] Similarly, the *rullepølser* now mostly use pork belly instead of mutton or beef sides, and is spiced with onion, peppercorns and allspice berries to make this ancient cooked, rolled meat.[145]

Vegetables, berries, jams, jellies, juices, beer and Akevitt: The probable reason few Norwegian Americans would think of vegetables as ethnic food is that by the time of mass emigration to America, the only vegetables — besides potatoes — cultivated in rural Norway were root crops and fava beans: *nepe* (turnip), *kålrot* (rutabaga) and *hestebønner* (horse beans).[146] Potatoes were introduced to Norway in the 18th century, and split peas, which were developed in Europe in the late 19th century, became a significant import just when a large part of the population was leaving for the U.S. Today Norway is still a major importer of peas, and *ertesuppe* (pea soup) and *ertestuing* (mashed peas) have become culinary staples served at springtime and Easter, complemented with pork, potatoes and carrots. It is frequently featured on the menus of Norwegian American fraternal organizations and cafes.[147]

Seeds found in the 9th-century Oseberg ship show that the Vikings must have grown cress, a sharp, spicy and fast-growing herb, and the ancient *Frostating* Law (1220-1250) contains language protecting growers of onions and angelica (an ancestor of the modern carrot) from thieves.[148] Early on, people gathered *sisselrot* (sweet-bitter ferns), *karvekål* (caraway sprouts) and *syregras* (sorrel) for culinary purposes, and *skjørbukgras* (scurvy grass) and other herbs for medicinal teas. The forest has always provided inexhaustible supplies of wild cherries, apples and various native berries, from *tyttebær* (cranberry), to *krekling* (crowberry), *heggebær* (choke cherry), *hyllebær* (elderberry), *enebær* (juniper berry), *molter* (cloudberry), *bringebær* (raspberry), *stikkelsbær* (gooseberry), *rips* (red currants), *jordbær* (strawberries), as well as *rabarbra* (rhubarb). Some of these, like crowberries and choke cherry, are rarely picked in the forests any more. In the case of strawberries, red currants (Lat. ribes alpinum) and gooseberries, the smaller, less productive native varieties were replaced by larger, improved cultivars and are now grown mostly in gardens or on industrial-scale farms. Another food gathered in the forests was *islandslav* (Iceland lichen, Lat. cetraria islandica). In 1939 Norwegian botanist Ove F. Arbo (1898-1993), recorded a recipe from Hardanger for cooking lichen in fresh milk and adding whey to make a cheese-like, salty curd.[149] In Sogn and Fjordane, *bresta mose* (curdled lichen) was eaten as a dessert sprinkled with sugar. Juniper berries, which ripen in their second year of growth, were used medicinally and to flavor game sauces. Juniper twigs, besides being burned for smoking meats, were boiled to produce an effective cleaner and hair wash. Boiled juniper water was also used in beer-making, and, diluted and sweetened with malt (a bi-product of beer making), it made a palatable drink.

As long as the making of jams and jellies was limited by the scarcity of sugar, people preserved the seasonal, wildcrafted fruits by cooking a kind of sour mash sweetened with honey. Cooking acidic fruit in the commonly used iron kettles, however, made the fruit black and bitter. Copper kettles were rare and aluminum pots did not become widely available until the 1915-1920s. Given those limitations, people turned to preservation methods no longer known today. As recently as fifty years ago, in northern Østerdalen, high-acid cranberries were placed in wooden tubs, covered with water and pressed down with a wooden lid. These were made into fruit porridge or soup. Another method was to crush some of the berries into juice and alternate layers of whole berries with juice. Lower-acid blueberries were topped by a layer of cranberries for longer keeping. Rhubarb stalks were split, leaving the ends in one piece so that the stalks could be hung on a line and dried. Juices and fruit soups were thickened with half-cooked, grated potatoes. Cloud berries, which have always enjoyed a special mystique among visitors to Norway, were placed in glass jars, covered with a tight lid and stored upside down in a cool cellar. The berries of the elder tree — considered holy in folk belief and often planted as *tuntre* (sacred tree placed at the center of the farm yard)[150] — were made into a medicinal juice. Chokecherries were processed into brandy by adding alcohol, filtering the juice a week later, and brining it with sugar. *Rødgrøt med fløte* (fruit soup with cream) continues to be a favorite dish among Norwegian Americans, and can be purchased as a prefabricated mix.

As the old saying goes, "there is food in good drink."[151] Beer and *Akevitt* (aquavit) and *mjød* (mead) are as old as Norwegian history, and although the production of alcoholic beverages in modern times has become a heavily taxed government monopoly, *hjemmebrent* (moonshine) is still quite common, made from raw materials "that range from sugar and water to mash made from potato or grains."[152] Løitens Export Aquavit, the best-known commercially made aquavit from Norway available in specialty stores in the U.S., is flavored with aniseed, caraway seeds, fennel, orange rind and oak. Beer was traditionally made from rye, although oats were used in a pinch. The grain was soaked in sacks placed in flowing water, or in wooden tubs thoroughly cleansed with *einelåg* (juniper wash), and then sprouted and dried in a special building heated with alder, and ground to prepare the malt for storage in anticipation of beer making. The actual brewing began with steeping the malt in water, preferably boiled juniper water, to give the beer deep flavor, dark color and keeping quality. The dried catkins of hops, grown in the farm garden, were added to lend the desired bitter flavor to the beer. The critical moment came when the yeast — usually preserved from previous brewings — was added. It was customary to "shout" to encourage the beer to become strong, while avoiding tramping feet or slamming a door, which would keep the beer from "going." The unfermented drink made from malt and hops before adding the yeast, was called *vørter* (vort). After yeasting, the beer was referred to as *tungøl* (heavy beer), and the process of fermentation took about 8-10 days. In the meantime, more juniper water was poured over the remaining malt to make *lettøl* (light beer), to which a little syrup was added to make a drink consumed during field work. As with *lefse*, there were about as many recipes for making beer as there were cultural regions in Norway. *Mjød* (mead) is another fermented drink, made from honey, water, hops, beer yeast, but without grain, and in modern times, is flavored with cinnamon, cloves, ginger and lemon. Once the water-honey mix comes to a boil, the hops and spices are added, and one third of the liquid is boiled off before the yeast is added, after cooling to body temperature. After three days, the brew is decanted into a barrel and corked and sealed. Before being tapped, the brew is finished by adding a bottle of white wine.

Continuity of Norwegian Tradition

As Norwegian American cultural historian Odd Lovoll writes, "Norway for most (immigrants) became the small rural community, the homestead, and the ancestral traditions in speech, food, and beliefs."[153] Norwegian immigrant folklore arose from the continuity of such traditions in the context of the new country, in which a large segment of Norway's population settled between the

1860s and 1930s. For a generation or two, Norwegian immigrants were able to maintain their self-identification with the world view, language, and material culture they had brought with them from their home districts in Norway, to the new communities they established on the American East Coast, the Midwest, and on the West Coast. Today, however, only a minority of Norwegian Americans still speak the language, or construe reality, or live in the material world, in the ways their immigrant ancestors did. This was, of course, to be expected. The self-sufficiency of farm or fishing homesteads, where survival depended on a close relationship to nature experienced as spiritually alive, has long since given way to industrially based livelihoods and to a modern, technologically and commercially based, world view.

Of course, the same thing happened in Norway itself. The process of agricultural industrialization which began by World War I, gathered speed by the 1930s, and led to a fundamental reorientation of the traditional rural culture of Norway, changing radically in response to local and world-wide economic developments.[154] Nevertheless, for decades Norway remained a relatively poor country. As recently as during the 1960s, when I was a student in Norway, people still spoke of *mangelkultur* (lean culture), expressing pride in making a good life from limited material resources. All that changed when oil was discovered on the North Sea continental shelf. In 1971 Norway became a major oil producer, and its culture rapidly shifted to a *forbrukskultur* (consumer culture),[155] like that of any other developed country. Today the average after-tax per capita income of Norwegians exceeds $50,000. This money is available for daily consumption because health care, retirement security, family subsidies in the form of 6-month paid new-parent leave (for each parent), childcare, month-long paid vacations, free primary and secondary education and similar benefits are provided from taxes, which expenditures amount to nearly fifty percent of GNP.[156] In addition, since the beginning of Norwegian oil exploration, the state has invested the public profit share of oil production in the global stock market. This "sovereignty fund" currently amounts to the tidy sum of 1 trillion dollars, which means that the Norwegian population of 5.3 million (0.06% of the world population), today owns 1.3% of the total global wealth held in stocks and shares, thus providing a nest egg of nearly $200,000 per capita in economic security. A concomitant change that has occurred since the turn of this century, and largely due to its economic success, is the ongoing redefinition of Norwegian ethnicity. In the last decades, the country has become home to increasing numbers of immigrants, foreign workers, and asylum-seekers from Europe, Asia, the Middle East and Africa, so that by 2018 immigrants constituted more than 17% of the population, almost the same share of immigrants relative to the total population as in the U.S.[157]

With the economic transformation of Norway from a system of independent, self-sufficient rural homesteads to a globalized economy based on industrial mass production, a degree of commercialization and mass production also occurred in Norwegian culture. An example of this shift is the growth of the widely popular summer festivals throughout Norway, presenting commercial artists performing art, theater, rock and classical music, and attracting audiences numbering in the tens of thousands. However, early on there also arose culturally significant counter-movements spearheaded by organizations such *Noregs Ungdomslag* (Norway's Youth Society) formed in 1896, which today has around 17,000 members and 450 local chapters. The society's activities are focused on cultivating the culture and language of pre-industrial, rural Norway through folk dance, dialect theater, crafts, and knowledge and use of *bunad*. From 1913 to 1956 the society was also closely tied to *Noregs Mållag* (Norway's Language Society), the organization promoting *nynorsk*. *Noregs Ungdomslag* has been a driving force for the building of *ungdomshus* (youth assembly houses), *kaffistova* (eateries) and *bondeheimar* (lodging houses for rural youth), folk high schools and secondary schools, and it has promoted *dugnad* (collective voluntary work).

The cultivation of *dugnad* is a social practice that ties the culture of modern Norway more closely to that of pre-industrial, rural society than any other modern practice. The Norwegian word *dugnad* derives from Old Norse *dugnaðr* (ability, help) and historically the term can be traced back to the close of the Viking Age, after the civil wars (1130-1240) between rival kings and pretenders to the throne of Norway ended. As a deeply held custom of communal work, the practice represented a traditional way of getting big tasks like haymaking and barn-raising done, usually followed by a big meal or feast. In a nation of farmers and fishermen, it functioned as a kind of community insurance. Similar practices have existed in most agricultural societies around the world. In the U.S., the practice is still common among the Amish, and latent forms of voluntary community work have recently re-emerged throughout America in the public response to the corona virus. Also, in 2013, the 380 lodges and 58,000 members of the Sons of Norway gave more than 500,000 hours of volunteer work and $1 million to their communities. In Norway, however, the *dugnad* tradition is also explicitly tied to the ideal of an inclusive economy, thus implementing the country's commitment to erasing social barriers relating to race, sexual orientation, and religion — a consideration that is particularly relevant to the global response to current racial inequality in the U.S. and elsewhere. According to the World Economic Forum, Norway tops all other nations as the most inclusive economy in the world. Today *dugnad* has come to mean universal voluntary work done for local, national and international causes, and the term has become so entrenched that in 2004 *dugnad* was voted Norway's "word of the year."[158] All members of society are expected to participate equally and with no regard to qualifications or social standing. In both rural and urban communities, *dugnad* focuses on the outdoors; for example, cleaning and restoring public parks, health centers, and even schools, anything that is not privately owned, and is usually practiced four times a year with the changing of the seasons, calling on people to collectively contribute to cleaning up the entire community, upcoming events being publicized ahead of time with posters and emails sent to every member of society. Embodying a culture of inclusiveness, *dugnad* strengthens the bonds of community, teaching that everybody matters and together people can make the world a better place. It comes as no surprise that in the time of the Covid pandemic, the Norwegian government explicitly calls upon the people to cooperate in the name of *dugnad*.

Given the interest today, both in Norway and in the U.S., in the cultural traditions of pre-industrial Norway, it is pertinent to ask: what does ethnicity mean to Norwegian Americans today and what is the continuity of Norwegian traditions currently found in America? It is interesting that in response to questions regarding Norwegian ethnicity for the present study, the answers went in three distinct directions: respondents either said that they thought of themselves as ethnic Norwegians because they were descendants of immigrants from Norway and looked the part in eye, hair and skin color; or that they cultivated Norwegian traditions going back to pre-industrial Norwegian culture in food ways, music, dancing, crafts or other aspects of material culture, because it reminded them of the culture of their immigrant forebears; or that, while not ethnic Norwegians genetically speaking, they had adopted aspects of Norwegian culture, mostly fiddle music, dancing, arts and crafts, because of their inherent artistic appeal. None of the respondents interviewed in 2020, however, still identified with the world view and folk beliefs documented among Norwegian Americans as recently as thirty years ago, if only as cultural memory. No one suggested that given their love of the folk traditions of late 19th century Norway, they yearned to return to the life style, the self-identification with nature, or the economic conditions that defined homestead life in pre-industrial Norway. Who would want to return to a subsistence life that required people to begin their daily work long before dawn and end it long after dark in the evening? Who would want to return to a life where individual self-fulfillment was secondary to family and community survival and health? So in spite of the fact that industrialization has brought us climate change, and the pollution of air, water and soil has created world wide health crises,[159] not many Norwegian Americans would suggest that we return to "the old days."

Another relevant consideration is that the language, food, crafts, clothing, dance and music traditions practiced by Norwegian Americans today give less of a true picture of life in rural communities in the past than they do of the hundred-year-old history of tradition programs of performance groups, museum exhibits, ethnic organizations, and educational institutions, as well as of commercial marketing.[160] Odd Lovoll argues that while Norwegian Americans "have evinced an exceptionally high degree of ethnocentricity, their sense of ethnicity has been severed from historical social structures," and instead has become "private," or "voluntary ethnicity," a reflection of what Max Weber has termed "subjective belief in a common descent."[161] It can also be said that in America ethnic identity has become to a large extent a matter of individual choice. So it is no surprise that the ethnic foods foregrounded by self-identified Norwegian Americans today, more often than not are industrially fabricated, imported products, rather than the traditional foods still occasionally produced by artisanal cooks and bakers from family traditions or cookbooks. Likewise, most of the *bunads* or simulations of "folk dress" worn by Norwegian Americans at festive occasions and weddings probably came from *Husfliden* or similar commercial craft outlets serving the domestic and foreign tourist trade. And the Viking-style boats made by the few Norwegian American boat builders in the U.S. mostly find their use in tourist activities or youth programs rather than meeting the needs of coastal fishermen who, historically, could not have survived without these superb vessels.

And yet these products serve an important cultural role in the ethnic communities, for example, in the Pacific Northwest. Norwegian Americans no longer live in tight-knit, self-sufficient, rural communities where their material and oral traditions served as strategies for daily survival in a harsh and demanding environment. However, Norwegian Americans appreciate the artifacts of the culture of the past for their unique fusion of function and form which they find beautiful and worthy of celebration and commemoration. Some, like silversmiths Lori Talcott and Felicia Bauer, while not of Norwegian descent, have internalized central aspects of Norwegian culture they express in decidedly idiosyncratic, modern forms. However, more than that, I believe, participation in folkloric events, dancing, fiddle playing, choral singing, crafts, cooking, baking and seasonal celebrations, affords Norwegian Americans in the Pacific Northwest and elsewhere a true sense of community that contemporary, commercially and technologically driven life, does not provide. Ethnic community, however tenuous and partial, provides a cultural home.

Informants

(in alphabetical order, immigrants listed as first generation Norwegian Americans, and so forth; unless otherwise noted, interviews, recordings and questionnaires are by the author):

Albers, Rosellen (3rd generation Norwegian American/ restoration artist/ Norwegian language student, LSI) — questionnaire, 2020.

Andresen, Øystein (1st generation Norwegian American/ retired pilot) — personal conversation, 2020.

Asheim, Paul (1st generation Norwegian American/ retired fisherman) — interview by Lars Jenner (UW student), 1990.

Bauer, Felicia (silversmith) — questionnaire, written communications and telephone conversations, 2020.

Berg, Lynn (4th generation Norwegian American/ violin & Hardanger fiddler maker) — telephone conversations & questionnaire, 2020.

Bloedel, Hans (UW graduate student) — recording, 1990.

Boyd, Bill (principal fiddle player for *Seattle Leikarringen)* — interview, recording, 2020.

Breivik, Lita (2nd generation Norwegian American/ retired registered dietician/ Norwegian language student, UW & SLI) — questionnaire, 2020.

Caspersen, Linda (1st generation Norwegian American/ Textile Curator & Collections Manager, Scandinavian Center, PLU) — questionnaire, written communications, telephone conversations, recording, 2020).

Edwards, Ella (1st generation Norwegian American) — Interview by Erik Christiansen (UW student), 1981.

Egerdahl, Ed (2nd generation Norwegian American/ Norwegian language teacher, Scandinavian Languages Institute (SLI), Seattle) — Conversations & questionnaire, 2020.

Ekenes, Eleanor (1st generation Norwegian American/ farmer/ UW student) — interview, 1982.

Floathe, Maury (2nd generation Norwegian American/ former UW student/ businessman) — questionnaire, 2020.

Hall, Anne (retired Lutheran pastor, Lopez Island / storyteller) — conversation, recording, 2020.

Harm, John (Norwegian American fisherman, retired) — interview by Lars Jenner, 1990.

Helding, John (3rd generation Norwegian American/ engineer / Lopez Island neighbor) — questionnaire, 2020.

Helsa, Erling (2nd generation Norwegian American/ semi-retired engineer/ Norwegian language student, SLI) — questionnaire, 2020.

Hilton, Peggy Lee (4th generation Norwegian American/ retired legal secretary/ Norwegian language student, SLI) — questionnaire, 2020.

Jacobs, Kurt (retired teacher, Lopez Island) — conversation, 2020.

Jangaard, Otto (1st generation Norwegian American/ retired fisherman) — interview by Lars Jenner, 1990.

Jenner, Lars (Swedish American/ extension lecturer, UW) — conversation, 2020.

Kaldahl, Jean. (Norwegian American) — Telephone conversation, 2020.

Kollé, Beth Sankey (5th generation Norwegian American/ folk dancer, musician & recording artist, author) — interview, questionnaire, and telephone conversations, 2020.

Kvistad, Jennell (4th generation Norwegian American/ grocer, Lopez Island) — interview & questionnaire, 2020.

Larson, A.K. (1st generation Norwegian American fisherman, retired/ member of Deep Sea Fishermen's Union/ advisor at UW Fisheries Research Institute, U.S. Bureau of Fisheries in Alaska, National Science Foundation in India) — interview by Barbara Rom (UW student), 1981.

Leander, Kristin (Swedish American) — telephone conversation, 2020.

"Letti" (last name not revealed/ 1st generation Norwegian American) — conversation, 1978.

Levenson, Martha (director of Lilla Spelmanslaget) — questionnaire, emails and telephone conversations, 2020.

Lillestol, Steven (4th generation Norwegian American/ miller, Lopez Island) — questionnaire & conversations, 2020.

Lokken, Harold (1st generation Norwegian American fisherman, retired/ manager of Vessel Owners' Association of Seattle — interviews by Henning Sehmsdorf & Lars Jenner, 1981.

Løklingholm, Gry (2nd generation Norwegian American/former UW student/ owner-manager, Trade Routes Forwarding) — interview, questionnaire, recording, 2020.

Losvar, Art (3rd generation Norwegian American/ boat builder) — interview by Henning Sehmsdorf & Gry Løklingholm, 1990.

Mauseth, Richard, M.D. (3rd generation Norwegian American/ pediatrician, retired/ Lopez Island neighbor) — questionnaire, 2020.

Mosness, Anne (2nd generation Norwegian American fisherwoman, retired/ conservationist, fisheries, maritime gender law & slow-food activist/ former president, American Maritime Association) — recording, 1990 / "Catch Curve" podcast interview by Robert E. Jones for *Seafoodie* (American Shoreline Podcast Network), 2020.

Nesvig, Rachel (5th generation Norwegian American/ Hardanger fiddle player, freelance musician) — questionnaire, 2020.

Olson, Anton (Norwegian American fisherman, retired) — interview by Barbara Rom, 1981.

Ostby, Gry (Roo) (4th generation Norwegian American/ grocer, Lopez Island) — questionnaire, 2020.

Patterson, Ann (5th or 6th generation Norwegian American/ retired registered nurse/ Norwegian language student, Sons of Norway & SLI) — questionnaire, 2020.

Peck, Solveig (4th generation Norwegian American/ retired owner-manager of interior design firm/ Norwegian language student, LSI) — questionnaire, 2020.

Pedersen, Einar (Norwegian American fisherman, retired) — interview by Barbara Rom, 1981.

Pedersen, Thrine (1st generation Norwegian American) — Interview by Joy Guttormsen, 1981.

Peterson, Larry (Norwegian Male Chorus, Bellingham) — telephone conversation, 2020.

Quistad, Kirsten (1st generation Norwegian American/ UW student) — interview, 1980; (storyteller and Norwegian language teacher) — interview, questionnaire & recording, 2020).

Reinert, Larry (2nd generation Norwegian American, folk dancer/ former president of *Leikarringen*) — interview & questionnaire, 2020.

Robertson, Darren (student, National Nordic Museum, Seattle) — questionnaire, 2020.

Ruud, Janet (3rd generation Norwegian American/ retired public school and community college teacher) — telephone conversations & questionnaire, 2020.

S. (full last name not revealed), Jim (Norwegian American fisherman, retired) — recorded, 1985.

Sather, David (4th generation Norwegian American/ former school principal, Lopez Island) — interview & questionnaire, 2020.

Schaumberg, Kenny (Loren) (former student, Huxley College for the Environment/ craftsman/ storyteller) — conversations, recording by Henning Sehmsdorf & Elizabeth Simpson, 2020.

Schweiss, Paul (3rd generation Norwegian American/ boat builder) — interview by Henning Sehmsdorf & Gry Løklingholm, 1990; telephone & email interviews, 2020).

Shaw, Frida (1st generation Norwegian American) — Interview by DyAnn Dennie, 1981.

Simonsen, Fred (1st generation Norwegian American; retired fisherman/ storyteller) — interviews & recording, 1990.

Smith, Jay (4th generation Norwegian American/ boat builder) — interview by Henning Sehmsdorf & Gry Løklingholm, 1990, 1992; questionnaire, interview & recording, 2020.

Sødal, Silje (2nd generation Norwegian American, Director of the North Urban Human Services Alliance) — questionnaire, 2020.

Swanson, Kari Gunvaldsen (4th generation Norwegian American/ semi-retired science researcher/ folkwear designer and producer) — questionnaire and telephone conversations, 2020).

Talcott, Lori (silversmith) — written communications and telephone conversations, 2020.

Waerness, Reitti (1st generation Norwegian American/ Lopez Island neighbor) — conversations, 2019-2020.

Weiberg, Erik W. (3rd generation Norwegian American/ Lutheran pastor, Ballard) — interview & questionnaire, 2020.

Interview Questionnaire, 2020:

Personal background:

Name:

Date of birth:

Place of Birth:

Current residence:

How long?

Profession?

If retired, since when?

What was the profession of your Norwegian forebears?

When did they arrive in the Pacific Northwest?

From Norway or from some other place in the U.S.?

Traditions:

Do you speak/read/write Norwegian?

If yes, where did you learn it?

If you have children, did you teach them Norwegian?

Do they speak it today?

Which Norwegian clubs, associations, groups do you belong to?

Do you participate in 17th of May celebrations? How?

Are you a Norwegian folk dancer? Since when?

Do you play a traditional instrument?

Do you sing Norwegian songs at home, in a choir, club or in church?

Do you know or tell any Norwegian jokes?

Do you know or tell any Norwegian stories, folktales, legends, personal experience narratives, belief stories (memorats)?

Where did you learn these stories? Where do you tell them?

Food ways:

Which traditional Norwegian foods do you buy?

Which traditional Norwegian foods do you prepare at home?

Where did you learn about Norwegian food ways?

Crafts:

Do you practice any traditional Norwegian crafts? Which?

Where did you learn it?

Are you currently teaching the craft? Where?

Lifestyle:

Do your house or furnishings reflect a Norwegian style?

Do you have or ride a Norwegian Fjord horse?

Do you practice Norwegian-style cross country skiing? Telemarking?

Do you build Norwegian-style wooden boats?

Do you use Norwegian-style wooden boats? Why?

Do you read about Norwegian-style wooden boats?

Belief traditions & practices:

Are you familiar with or hold traditional Norwegian beliefs surrounding the human soul, alternative healing practices, relations of the dead and the living, protective amulets, nature spirits, the "invisible folk," trolls, or other supranormal beings?

Do you practice a religion? Which?

Are you a member of a church?

Did you ever hear/participate in a church service held in Norwegian? Where? When?

Are there any Norwegian sayings or rituals practiced in your own life? Daily?
On special occasions?

Do you practice any special Norwegian customs at Christmas? Easter?
Midsummer?

Other?
Add extra pages, if desired.

End Notes:

Settlement, Assimilation & Adaptation (pp. 5-10)

1 This essay is an updated and much expanded version of an article published as "Assimilation, Adaptation, Survivals: Norwegian-American Traditions in the Pacific Northwest," *Northwest Folklore,* 1988, vol. 7, no. 1: 3-13; in Norwegian as "Assimilasjon og tilpasning. Norsk-amerikanske tradisjoner på den amerikanske vestkysten," *Tradisjon,* 1989, 75-84.

2 Patsy H. Hegstad 1985. "Scandinavian Settlements in Seattle," *Norwegian-American Studies*, vol. 30: 55-74. See also Sverre Arestad 1985. "Norwegians in the Pacific Coast Fisheries," op.cit., 96-129, and Jorgen Dahlie 1967. "A Social History of Scandinavian Immigration, Washington State, 1895-1910." (Ph.D. diss., Washington State U.), passim.

3 Odd S. Lovoll 1998. *The Promise Fulfilled: A Portrait of Norwegian Americans Today.* U. of Minnesota Press, 2 & 49.

4 Egerdahl (informant), 2020.

5 Weiberg (informant), 2020.

6 Odd S. Lovoll 1977. "Cultural Pluralism vs. Assimilation: The Views of Valdemar Ager." *Norwegian-American Historical Association,* 25-26.

7 Quistad (informant), 2020.

8 Thrine Pedersen (informant), 1981; Ekenes (informant), 1982.

9 Quistad (informant), 2020.

Storied Tradition (pp. 10-28):

10 See Gerald Cashion 1974. "Folklore, Kinesiological Folklore, and the Macro-Folklore Context," in: Gerald Cashion (ed.) 1974. *Conceptual Problems in Contemporary Folklore Study.* U. of Indiana Press, 24-35.

[11] See "Good Friends and Neighbors," and "The Spirit of the Farm,' in: Reimund Kvideland & Henning K. Sehmsdorf 1988. *Scandinavian Folk Belief and Legend.* U. of Minnesota Press, 222-252.

[12] Paul Harrison 1996. "North American Indians: the Spirituality of Nature." (https://www.pantheism.net/paul/history/native-americans.htm). Retrieved May 3, 2020.

[13] Laura Bland 2017. "Betwixt nature and God dwelt the medieval 'preternatural'." (https://aeon.co/ideas/betwixt-nature-and-god-dwelt-the-medieval-preternatural). Retrieved May 3, 2020.

[14] John Smith 1635. "New England," in: J. Baird Callicott 2020. "The Puritan Origins of the American Wilderness Movement." https://nationalhumanitiescenter.org/tserve/nattrans/ntwilderness/essays/puritan.htm. Retrieved May 3, 2020.

[15] Lovoll, 1998, 21.

[16] On the attitude of the church concerning healers and other people employing supranormal powers, see "Healers and Wise Folk," in: Kvideland & Sehmsdorf, op.cit., 122-155, and "Witchcraft," in: ibid, 157-200 (especially legend no. 42.1). For a folktale illustrating the tenuous social role of the parson, see "The Boy and the Parson" (AT 1535), in: Reimund Kvideland & Henning K. Sehmsdorf 1999. *All The World's Reward: Folktales Told by Five Scandinavian Storytellers.* U. of Washington Press, no. 345. About the dissonance between traditional and church-sponsored attitudes concerning marital sexuality and conception, see Henning K. Sehmsdorf 1989. "AT 711 The Beautiful and the Ugly Twin: The Tale and its Sociocultural Context," *Scandinavian Studies*, vol. 61: 339-352.

[17] Ole Rölvaag 1927. *Giants in the Earth.* A.L. Burt Co., 107.

[18] Ekenes (informant), 1982.

[19] Rölvaag, op.cit., 64-65; see also Lilly Weiser-Aall 1965. "En studie om vardøyger" (A Study About the Vardøyger), *Norveg*, vol. 12: 73-112.

[20] Shaw (informant), 1981.

[21] Kvideland & Sehmsdorf, 1988, 41-81.

22 Edwards (informant), 1981. See also Henning K. Sehmsdorf 1988. "Envy and Fear in Scandinavian Folk Tradition: Belief and Genre," *Ethnologia Scandinavica: A Journal for Nordic Ethnology,* 34-42.

23 "Lettie" (informant), 1978.

24 Edwards (informant), 1981.

25 Bente Alver & Torunn Solberg, 1998. "Alternative Medicine in Today's Society," in: Reimund Kvideland & Henning K. Sehmsdorf 1998. *Nordic Folklore: Recent Studies.* Indiana U. Press, 207-220. See also Bente Alver & B. af Klintberg, A.-L. Siikala, B. Rörby 1980. *Botare: En bok om etnomedisin i Norden* (Healers: A Book About Ethno-Medicine in the Nordic Countries). Institutet för folklivsforskning vid Nordiska Museet & Stockholm U.

26 Larson (informant), 1981.

27 E. Pedersen (informant), 1981.

28 Olson (informant), 1981.

29 Søldal (informant), 2020.

30 Lillestol (informant), 2020.

31 See, for example, Mary Norton 1952. *The Borrowers.* Dent; see also Henning K. Sehmsdorf 1995. "Folksagan i klassrummet" (The Folktale in the Classroom), in: Gun Herranen 1995. *Sagorna finns överallt: Perspektiv på folksagan i samhället* (You Will Find Folktales Everywhere: Perspectives on the Folktale in Society), Nordic Institute of Folklore, no. 28. Carlssons Bokförlag, 203-218.

32 Albers (informant), 2020.

33 Patterson (informant), 2020.

34 Bloedel (informant), 1990.

35 Jan Harold Brunvand 1960. "Thor, the Cheechako and the Initiates' Tasks: A Modern Parallel for an Old Jest," in *Southern Folklore Quarterly,* vol. 24: 235-238.

36 Hall (informant), 2020.

37 Herbert J. Gans 2010. "Symbolic Ethnicity: The Future of Ethnic Groups and Cultures in America." (https://doi.org/10.1080/01419870.1979.9993248). Retrieved April 12, 2020.

38 See Henry J. Cadbury 1825. "The Norwegian Quakers of 1825," *Harvard Theological Review,* October, 1925; quoted in *Norwegian-American Studies,* vol. 1: 60ff.

39 See Sandra K.D. Stahl 1983. "Personal Experience Stories," in: Richard Dorson, 1983. *Handbook of American Folklore.* U. of Indiana Press, 268-276.

40 On the style of Norwegian folktales, compare the discussion of Olav Eivindsson Austad ("Norway's Last Great Storyteller"), whose stories were collected during the same time period Simonsen describes in his repertoire, in: Kvideland & Sehmsdorf 1999, 13-22.

41 The tape recordings of Simonsen's stories and accompanying photographs are held by the Nordic Heritage Museum, Seattle. For a fuller discussion of Fred Simonsen's life and his storytelling, see Henning K. Sehmsdorf 1991. "I Went Through a Lot of Misery: The Stories of Fred Simonsen, Norwegian American Fisherman," *Northwest Folklore,* vol. 10, no. 1: 5-42.

42 Kvideland & Sehmsdorf, 1988, 21.

43 Jacobs (informant), 2020.

44 Probably the Fly Amanita *(Amanita mascara),* see David Arora 1991. *All that The Rain Promises and More...* Ten Speed Press, 77.

45 See "The Human Soul," in: Kvideland & Sehmsdorf 1988, 38-81, especially legend no. 9.1 ("How to Reveal your Character").

46 Schaumberg (informant), 2020.

47 Quistad (informant), 2020.

48 See "The Invisible Folk," in: Kvideland & Sehmsdorf, 1988, 201-275.

49 Lauri Honko 1964. "Memorates and the Study of Folk Belief," *Journal of the Folklore Institute,* vol. 1: 5-19; reprinted in: Kvideland & Sehmsdorf, 1998, 100-109.

50 Caspersen (informant), 2020. Compare Kvideland & Sehmsdorf, 1988, 20ff.

Dancing, Instrumental Music, Choral Singing (pp. 28-42):

51 Cashion, ibid.

52 In 2005, however, Norwegian American fiddler Karen Solgård was invited to perform on the Hardanger Fiddle in Faith Lutheran Church in Isanti, Minnesota — the very heartland of Norwegian America. How times change! See *Isanti County News*, 2005 (http://www.isanticountynews.com/2005/november/ 23fiddle.html). Retrieved May 15, 2020.

53 See "The Water Sprite," and legends no. 51.1-3, in: Kvideland & Sehmsdorf, 1988, 252-259. See also Sverre Sandvik 1983. *Vi Byggjer Hardingfele: Ei bok om felebygging med malar i naturleg storleik* (We Build Hardanger Fiddles: A Book About Building Hardanger Fiddles with Templates in Actual Size). Tiden, 12-13.

54 This legendary event was memorialized by tradition collector and minister, Jørgen Moe, in his ballad "*Fanitullen*" (1850). For the "demonic" sound of the Hardanger fiddle, see Patrice George 2008. "Knut Hamre and Benedicte Maurseth — Rosa I Botnen." (Knut Hamre & Benedicte Maurseth — Essential Rosa). *RootsWorld* 26. (http://www.rootsworld.com/reviews/botnen06.shtml). Retrieved May 20, 2020.

55 Bjørnstjerne Bjørnson, *Arne* (1859), in: Bjørnstjerne Bjørnson 1963. *Bondefortellinger* (Peasant Stories). Gyldendal, 118ff (translation mine). For further discussion of the numinous aura of the fiddler and his ambiguous social role in traditional Norwegian society, see Henning K. Sehmsdorf 1969. "Bjørnson's 'Trond' and Popular Tradition," *Scandinavian Studies*, vol. 41, no. 1: 56-66.

56 See "The Lutheran Identity," in: Lovoll, 1998, 19-23.

57 Levenson (informant), 2020.

58 See Garborg, Hulda 1913. *Songdansen i Nordlandi* (Song Dances in the North). Aschehoug.

59 Seattle Lilla Spelmanslag, 2020. https://www.seattlelillalag.org/. Retrieved May 15, 2020.

[60] Boyd (informant), 2020.

[61] Jens Lund (in collaboration with Elizabeth Simpson) 1989. *Folk Arts of Washington State.* Washington State Folklife Council, 62-63.

[62] Berg (informant), 2020.

[63] See Margaret M. Miller & Sigmund Aarseth 1974. *Norwegian Rosemaling: Decorative Painting on Wood.* Scribners.

[64] Peterson (informant), 2020.

[65] See Hildegard M. Strom 2018. "A Brief History of Sons of Norway." (https://www.sofn.com/about_us/showPage.jsp?document=History.html). Retrieved June 15, 2020.

[66] See "Sons of Norway, 1895-2020." (http://www.sonjax.com/). Retrieved June 15, 2020.

[67] See Lovoll 1998, 1.

[68] Kaldahl (informant), 2020. See also Norwegian Ladies Chorus of Seattle, 2020. (https://www.nlcofseattle.org/). Retrieved June 16, 2020.

[69] See Storlosjen Døtre av Norge Paa Pacific-Kysten (Grand Lodge, Daughters of Norway on the Pacific Coast) 1923. *Sange med Musikk og Tekst til Bruk ved Passende Anledninger* (Songs and Texts for Use at Appropriate Occasions); *Songbook,* 2nd edition, 1967; *Songbook,* 3rd edition. 2018. Grand Lodge, Daughters of Norway.

Husflid: Weaving, Knitting, Lace Making (pp. 42-61):

[70] Peck (informant), 2020.

[71] Øystein Andresen (informant, 2020), for example, proudly displays in his home an upright clock carved in traditional eucanthus style by his wife's immigrant father in the 1960s.

[72] Ruud (informant), 2020.

[73] See Kvideland & Sehmsdorf, 1999, 4-5.

74 For a discussion of the role of *husflid* in the socio-economic and cultural context of pre-industrial, rural Norway, and its replacement by leisure-time interest in folk crafts, see Kristofer Visted & Hilmar Stigum 1971. *Vår gamle bondekultur* (Our Old Rural Culture). 3rd ed. Cappelen, vol. I, 309-384.

75 Kollé (informant), 2020. For a description of various spinning wheel designs, see "The Anatomy of a Spinning Wheel: Parts of a Spinning Wheel & How it Works." https://midnightyarn.com/spinning/spinning-wheel-anatomy-how-it-works/. Retrieved July 31, 2020.

76 See "Iron Age tunic found in Norway glacier recreated." http://www.thehistoryblog.com/archives/33671. Retrieved July 31, 2020.

77 Caspersen (informant), 2020.

78 See https://annemor.com/english/. Retrieved August 1, 2020.

79 Terri Shea 2007. *Selbuvotter* (Selbu Mittens). *Biography of a Knitting Tradition.* Spinningwheel.

80 Roald Wenche & Annichen Sibbern Bøhn 1929. *Norwegian Knitting Designs - 90 Years Later: A New Look at the Classic Collection of Scandinavian Motifs and Patterns.* Trafalgar Square Books.

81 Lund, op.cit, 30.

82 http://www.lacemakers.org/about-lacemaking. Retrieved July 31, 2020.

83 Lori Talcott is a Seattle silversmith who apprenticed in Norway. See https://www.loritalcott.com/about-1. Retrieved July 31, 2020.

84 Kollé (informant), 2020.

85 See *Norsk institutt for bunad og folkedrakt* (Norwegian Institute for *Bunad* and Folk Costumes). https://bunadogfolkedrakt.no/historikk. Retrieved May 2020.

86 https://www.sustainableballard.org/about/. Retrieved August 10, 2020.

87 N.W. Damm, 1998.

88 Talcott (informant), 2020.

Jewelry (pp. 61-71):

89 https://hildesolv.no/. Retrieved August 30, 2020. See also Hilde K. Nødtvedt, 2014. *"Kvar sølvsmed sitt mot:" om kreativitet og variabilitet i det norske draktsølvet* ("Every silversmith according to her spirit:" About Creativity and Variability in Norwegian Costume Jewelry). Published Master's thesis. Høgskolen i Telemark Fakultet for Tradisjonskunst (University School for Traditional Arts in Telemark).

90 https://www.mindat.org/loc-33366.html. Retrieved August 30, 2020).

91 The range of talismanic protections and aids by means of metal amulets and rituals involving silver and steel included most aspects of farm life: for example, securing aid in childbirth and protection of the unbaptized newborn; binding the water sprite who might drown the children; siphoning milk, beer, brandy from a knife stuck in a wooden wall; identifying witch butter by sticking a steel blade into it; healing illness by shooting silver bullets over the sick; shooting silver pellets into a dead man to keep him from leaving the grave. See Kvideland & Sehmsdorf 1988, passim.

92 See "The Invisible Folk," in: Kvideland & Sehmsdorf, 1988, 201-275.

93 Ibid, legends no. 50.1-50.5.

94 See Eivind Tveiten 1955. "Bunadsylvet," in: *Telemarksbunader. Nedervde kledeskikkar for menn og kvinner* (Telemark *Bunad*: Traditional Dress Customs for Men and Women). Telemark Husflidssentral (Telemark Center for Home Crafts) & Mittet.

95 Jorunn Fossberg 1991. *Draktsølv* (Dress Silver), Universitetsforlaget, 66-67.

96 See Dana Standish's 1996 article on Lori Talcott's work in *Metalsmith Magazine*. https://www.ganoksin.com/article/lori-talcott-large-life/. Retrieved August 30, 2020.

97 https://www.loritalcott.com/traditional-work. N.d. Retrieved August 30, 2020.

98 http://www.seattlemetalsguild.org/wp-content/uploads/2017/08/Lori-Talcott-Qualifications-791x1024@2x.pdf. Retrieved August 31, 2020.

99 James G. Frazer 1951. *The Golden Bough*. Macmillan, 43.

100 See Kvideland & Sehmsdorf, 1988, passim; see also Bente Alver, 1980.

101 Talcott, op.cit. See also Talcott 2009. "The Norwegian *Bolesølje*: A Microcosm of Medieval Aesthetics and Belief." Unpublished paper.

102 https://siennapatti.com/project/special-project-lori-talcott-homeopathic-objects-part-1-july-24-august-16-2015/. Retrieved September 1, 2020.

103 Freya (or Frea) is called *ælmihtig* (all-powerful) in "Caedmon's Hymn" from Bede's *Ecclesiastical History of England* (597 A.D.); in Snorri's *Prose Edda* (1320 A.D.), Freyja claims half the heroes slain on the battlefield for herself; she is said to own *Brísingamen* (necklace of the Brisings), and be able to change herself into a falcon; in the 13th century *Poetic Edda*, Freyja is called the goddess of love and a sybil. *Brísingamen* is also mentioned in the Anglo-Saxon epic poem *Beowulf* (between 700-1000 A.D.) The name of the necklace has been tentatively derived from Old Norse *brísingr*, a poetic term for "fire" or "amber," combined with *men*, meaning necklace or torc.

104 Talcott (informant), 2020.

105 Bauer (informant), 2020. For a discussion of variability and creativity within the bounds of *sølje* tradition, see Nødtvedt, op.cit: 8, 64-72.

106 Christian Norberg-Schulz 1979. *Genius Loci: Towards a Phenomenology of Architecture*. Rizolli.

107 https://snohetta.com/about. Retrieved September 12, 2020.

108 Bauer (informant), 2020.

Boat Building (pp. 71-77):

109 Gry Løklingholm 1992. "Survival and Revival: The Traditions of Scandinavian American Boatbuilding Around Puget Sound," *Northwest Folklore*, vol. 10, no. 2: 24-41.

110 For the distinction between conservatism and dynamism in folkloric transmission, see Barre Toelken 1979. *The Dynamics of Folklore*. Houghton Mifflin, 35.

111 George H. Schoemaker (ed.) 1990. *The Emergence of Folklore in Everyday Life*. Trickster Press, 133.

[112] Løklingholm, op.cit., 40.

Food Ways (pp. 78-96):

[113] Magnus Nilsson 2015. *The Nordic Cook Book*. Phaidon, 12.

[114] See Hjalmar Stigum 1965. "Norsk matskikk" (Norwegian Food Customs), in: Olga Ambjørnrud et al. (eds.) 1965. *Norsk mat* (Norwegian Food). Cappelen, 9-16.

[115] Berg, Kollé, Quistad, Egerdahl, Patterson, Albers, Weiberg, Breivik, Schweiss, Swanson, Smith, Caspersen, Kvistad, a.o. (informants), 2020.

[116] Reinert, Egerdahl, Patterson, Levinson, Breivik, Nesvig, Hesla, Søldal, Peck, Ruud, Lillestøl, a.o. (informants), 2020.

[117] Stigum, ibid.

[118] See Elisabeth Moe 1965. "Året rundt i hverdag og helg" (The Annual Round of Everyday and Holidays), 1965, in: Ambjørnrud, op.cit, 17-48.

[119] See Anders Grønli & Elisabeth Moe 1965. "Fisk" (Fish), in: Ambjørnrud, op.cit, 206-236.

[120] Stigum, op.cit, 27.

[121] Ambjørnrud, op.cit., 225.

[122] Ibid, 223.

[123] Henning K. Sehmsdorf 2014. "The Staff of Life? The Culture of Gluten Intolerance as Seen Through the Eyes of a Homestead Baker." *Biodynamics*, Fall 2014, 35-37. (http://sshomestead.org/wp-content/uploads/Sehmsdorf%20article%20from%20Fall%202014%20Biodynamics.pdf). Retrieved June 25, 2020.

[124] See Johanne Jansen 1965. "Bakverk" (Baked Goods), in: Ambjørnrud, op.cit., 113-156.

[125] Nilsson, op.cit, 547.

[126] Ibid, 605.

[127] Ibid, 547.

128 Stigum, op.cit., 447.

129 See Reidar T. Christiansen 1946. *Folktales of Norway.* Transl. by Pat Shaw Iversen. U. of Chicago Press.

130 See Kvideland & Sehmsdorf, 1988, 237-238; Kvideland & Sehmsdorf, 1999, 84-85.

131 "Brunost" 2020. https://en.wikipedia.org/wiki/Brunost. Retrieved June 5, 2020; see also Arne Espelund 1998. *Brunosten, historien til et godt næringsemne gjennom 300 år* (Brown Cheese: The History of a Good Food Stuff over 300 Years). Arketype.

132 See Johanne Jansen & Elisabeth Moe 1965. "Melk og Ost" (Milk and Cheese), in: Ambjørnrud, op.cit., 49-95.

133 Nancy T. Maar 2004. "Jarlsberg's Stamford, Conn. Importer Eyes U.S. Growth." Knight Ridder/Tribune Business News. (https://web.archive.org/web/20140808120159/http://www.highbeam.com/doc/1G1-118420937.html). Retrieved June 7, 2020.

134 See "The Invisible Folk," in: Kvideland & Sehmsdorf, 1988, 205-280, especially legends nos. 45.6, 46.1 (legend type ML6000), 46.2 , 46.7, 47.5 (legend type ML 6025), and 47.13 (legend type ML 6055).

135 See "Stealing Milk," in: ibid, 171-179, legends no. 38.1-39.5. See also end note 21, above.

136 Nilsson, op.cit., 72.

137 Ibid, 69.

138 Ibid, 74.

139 Ambjørnrud, op.cit, 80.

140 Anders Grønli & Elisabeth Moe 1965. "Kjøtt" (Meat), in: Ambjørnrud, 1965, op.cit., 157-205.

141 Tom Seymour 2017. "Are Organ Meats Good for You?" *Medical News Today.* https://www.medicalnewstoday.com/articles/319229. Retrieved June 3, 2020.

142 Nilsson, op.cit, 425.

143 Ibid, 430.

[144] Ibid, 432.

[145] Ibid.

[146] See Jansen & Moe 1965. "Grønnsaker, bær og frukt" (Vegetables, Berries and Fruit), in: Ambjørnrud, 1965, op.cit., 246-258.

[147] "Norwegian Pea Soup." (https://www.sofn.com/norwegian_culture/recipe_box/soups/norwegian_pea_soup/). Retrieved June 15, 2020.

[148] "Frostatingsloven" (The Frostating Law) 1200. (https://web.archive.org/web/20071030115308/http://www.arkivverket.no/webfelles/skrift-i-tusenaar/middelalderen/storlink4.htm). Retrieved June 12, 2020.

[149] Jansen & Moe, op.cit., 256.

[150] See Henning K. Sehmsdorf. "The Poetry of Halldis Moren Vesaas & Tradition," in: Leif Mæhle (ed.) 1987. *Halldis Moren Vesaas: Festskrift til 80-årsdagen 18. November 1987* (Halldis Moren Vesaas: Congratulatory Publication on her 80th Birthday, 18 November 1987). Aschehoug, 132-140.

[151] Quoted in Ambjørnrud, 1965, op.cit., 261.

[152] Nilsson, op.cit., 716.

Continuity of Norwegian Tradition (pp. 96-101):

[153] Lovoll, 1998, 3.

[154] See Sehmsdorf, ibid.

[155] Marte Klavenes 2004. *Klær og miljø* (Clothes and Milieu). Master's thesis, NTNU (Norwegian University of Science and Technology), 7.

[156] Based on "World Economic Outlook Databook of the International Monetary Fund," IMF 2020. https://en.wikipedia.org/wiki/List_of_countries_by_government_spending_as_percentage_of_GDP. Retrieved June 15, 2020.

[157] For a personal perspective on immigration to Norway and its socio-economic costs, see Elizabeth Simpson & Henning Sehmsdorf 2019. *Last Trip to Germany: Reflections on Art, Culture, Economics, History, Family and Travel in the Age of Climate Change 2018*. S&S Homestead Press, 35.

158 See "Worklife" 2018. www.bbc.com/worklife/article/20180521-how-dugnad...) Retrieved June 11, 2020.

159 See Henning K. Sehmsdorf 1974. "'Everyday Myths and Dystopia: Axel Jensen's *Epp.* Science Fiction as Social Satire," PNCFL (Pacific Northwest Council on Foreign Languages), vol. XXV, no. 1: 118-121.

160 Tone Erlien & Egil Bakka 2017. "Museums, Dance, and the Safeguarding of Intangible Cultural Practice." *Santander Art and Culture Law Review*, vol. 2: 135-156; Bakka 2015. "Safeguarding of Intangible Cultural Heritage — the Spirit and the Letter of the Law," *Musikk og Tradisjon* (Music & Tradition), vol. 29: 135-169. See also Barbara Kirshenblatt-Gimblett 2004. "Intangible Heritage as Meta-Cultural Production," *Museum International*, vol. 56, no. 1-2: 52-65.

161 Lovoll, op.cit, 179 & 214; Richard D. Alba 1990. *Ethnic Identity: The Transformations of White America.* Yale U. Press, 313.